Cross-Country Ski Socks on loom, Vesterheim Museum. PHOTOGRAPH BY SUE FLANDERS

NORWEGIAN HANDKNITS

HEIRLOOM DESIGNS FROM VESTERHEIM MUSEUM

SUE FLANDERS AND JANINE KOSEL

Voyageur Press

First published in 2009 by Voyageur Press, an imprint of MBI Publishing Company, 400 First Avenue North, Suite 300, Minneapolis, MN 55401 USA

The information in this book is true and complete to the best of our knowledge. All recommendations are made without any guarantee on the part of the author or Publisher, who also disclaims any liability incurred in connection with the use of this data or specific details.

We recognize, further, that some words, model names, and designations mentioned herein are the property of the trademark holder. We use them for identification purposes only. This is not an official publication.

Voyageur Press titles are also available at discounts in bulk quantity for industrial or sales-promotional use. For details write to Special Sales Manager at MBI Publishing Company, 400 First Avenue North, Suite 300, Minneapolis, MN 55401 USA.

To find out more about our books, visit us online at www.voyageurpress.com.

Editor: Kari Cornell
Designer: Elly Rochester
Schematics and charts: Barbara Drewlo

Printed in the United States of America

Library of Congress Cataloging-in-Publication Data

Flanders, Sue, 1960-

Norwegian handknits : heirloom designs from Vesterheim Museum / Sue Flanders and Janine Kosel ; photos by Sue Flanders.

    p. cm.

ISBN 978-0-7603-3428-7 (plc)

 1. Knitting—Patterns. 2. Knitting—Norway. I. Kosel, Janine, 1964- II. Vesterheim Norwegian-American Museum. III. Title.

TT825.F556 2009

746.43'2041—dc22

        2008052986

On the cover: Norwegian Knapsack, photograph by Sue Flanders

On the frontispiece: Rosemaled Bag with Shag, photograph by Sue Flanders

On the title pages: Main image: Cross Country Ski Socks, photograph by Sue Flanders; Inset image: Hillside scene, probably Hardanger, Norway, 1890s. *Senator Knute Nelson Collection, Vesterheim Archive*

On the back cover: All photographs by Sue Flanders

About the Authors

SUE FLANDERS has been designing knitwear for more than twenty years. Her patterns have appeared in many publications, including *Interweave Knits*, *Knitter's* magazine, and *Cast-On*, and in two books by Melanie Falick, *Knitting America* and *Kids Knitting*. Sue lives in the Twin Cities area.

JANINE KOSEL is an accomplished knitter who has studied under greats like Alice Starmore, Meg Swansen, and Candice Eisner Strict. Janine works at Three Kitten's Needle Arts in Mendota Heights and teaches knitting and tatting workshops at many Minneapolis- and St. Paul–area knitting and needlework shops.

This book is dedicated to our mothers,
Rosemary Jane Malkovich Kosel and Margaret Viola Dye Klein

"We honor our mothers with all they have taught us."
ENID GRINDLAND

Contents

Vesterheim Museum, today.

oreword

by Laurann Gilbertson, Textile Curator
Vesterheim Norwegian-American Museum

Museum collections are meant to be shared in formal exhibitions, studied through careful research, and preserved for future generations. Museum collections are also for inspiration. All museum curators hope our artifacts will inspire visitors to want to learn more about history, culture, art, craftsmanship, and technology—and about themselves. Vesterheim's collections inspired Sue Flanders and Janine Kosel to create the patterns that appear in this book. It has been my pleasure to watch as they discovered our textile treasures, knit reproductions, and created new interpretations.

The Norwegian word *flink* describes Sue and Janine very well. *Flink* is hard to express in a single English word. It means adroit, clever, creative, ingenious, skillful, resourceful, and gifted. Their joyful and artistic designs honor and celebrate history, tradition, and needleworkers.

I hope you will follow the thread set forth in this book. Be inspired, add some of yourself to your work, and do what you love.

*Woman's embroidered shirt,
from East Telemark, Norway, eighteenth century.*
LUTHER COLLEGE COLLECTION

A Brief History of Vesterheim Norwegian-American Museum

The collection that would become Vesterheim Norwegian-American Museum started in 1877 as a study aid for students at Luther College in Decorah, Iowa, and now includes twenty-four thousand objects. The first gift to the museum was a collection of bird eggs and nests. In the early years, the collection included natural history (biology, geology) and cultural items, some of which had been collected by Lutheran missionaries serving around the globe.

By 1895, faculty and alumni at Luther College officially resolved that Norwegian immigrant materials should be a stated focus of the collection. The museum became a pioneer in the preservation and promotion of America's cultural diversity. It was a natural repository for items that might otherwise have been thrown away.

The first historic building was added to the grounds in 1913, starting the Open Air Division. No other museum in the United States was collecting buildings, though this was already taking place in Scandinavia. Skansen, in Stockholm, Sweden, and Norsk Folkemuseum in Oslo, Norway, were the world's first open-air museums.

In 1925, in honor of one hundred years of emigration, Anders Sandvig, founder of Maihaugen Open Air Museum, Lillehammer, Norway, coordinated a gift of artifacts from Norwegian museums to the collection at the Luther College Museum. "May these objects work," wrote Sandvig, "so that the Norwegian-ness in you will not die too soon, and the connection with the homeland will because of this be stronger. Receive this gift as proof that we follow you all in our hearts, even though the big Atlantic parts us."

The artifacts, which took two years to assemble and filled twenty-three crates, included roomfuls of carved and painted Norwegian furniture and household items like ale bowls, trunks, and cooking equipment. The gift also included many stunning textiles, like the embroidered shirt from Telemark that inspired the Foolish Virgins Pillow. The museum in Nordmøre, Norway, sent several clothing items, including two men's shirts trimmed with fine whitework embroidery. Those who made the donation had no way of knowing that this gift meant the survival of several cultural treasures because their museum would be destroyed during World War II.

After the war, Inga Bredesen Norstog, curator of what was now called the Norwegian-American Historical Museum (still part of Luther College), submitted articles about the museum to newspapers and magazines around the country, which were published in the *New York Times, Chicago Sunday Tribune, Life, Woman's Day, Antiques*, and some national Norwegian-language publications. Sometimes she would feature specific artifacts, which then made people think about how special some of their family pieces were. Soon the museum was receiving visitors and artifact donations from all over the United States.

The museum became an independent institution in 1964 and adopted the name Vesterheim in honor of the term that immigrants used to describe America in letters home. America was their *vesterheim*, their "western home."

In the 1960s, Director Marion Nelson added fine art to the museum's collection statement, reflecting his belief that there is art in everyday objects. Today, we are "refining" the collection, looking to fill gaps to ensure that Vesterheim's artifacts can tell more stories of immigrant experiences, of American experiences.

Norwegian and Norwegian-American Knitting

Historically, knitting was a vital skill in Norway. Women used wool that they had processed, beginning with raising sheep, shearing them, carding the wool, and spinning it into yarn. Many Norwegian immigrants living in the American Midwest in the nineteenth century also raised sheep for their warm, soft, durable wool and for meat.

Although immigrant women could have purchased ready-knit items or yarn for knitting, they often processed their own wool for yarn. Immigrants believed that hand-spun wool yarn and hand-knit objects were better—warmer and more durable—than what they could buy in the store. If women had not brought spinning wheels with them, they could buy them here from talented carpenters or even from mail-order businesses, such as Alfred Andresen & Company of Minneapolis, Minnesota, who imported wheels from Norway.

Aside from warmth and durability, knitting was also valued for its beauty. Colorfully embroidered mittens and gloves were worn to church in Norway.

Hillside scene, probably Hardanger, Norway, 1890s.
SENATOR KNUTE NELSON COLLECTION, VESTERHEIM ARCHIVE

Margit Kostveit carding (left), her son Halvor, and her sister spinning. Gardsjord, Rauland, Telemark, Norway, 1890s.
GAUSTA COLLECTION, VESTERHEIM ARCHIVE

The Norwegian sweaters that we love so much (and need in cold climates) have very humble beginnings. Some of the earliest sweaters, worn by men, were considered underwear. The sweaters were worn over a shirt and tucked into trousers, with a vest and coat worn over the top. This is why you don't see sweaters often in old photographs unless, as in the photograph by Herbjørn Gausta of Gjermund Gaustad on page 10, one of the outer layers has been removed.

Many of these sweaters featured two-color designs because of the extra warmth the second yarn provided, but because the undershirt/sweaters were tucked into trousers, the sweaters featured only one color below the waist to save time and conserve yarn.

Luckily for us, Norwegian sweaters became outerwear for everyone, young and old. For some, sweaters like Sue and Janine's Voss Sweater have become a palette for creative expression, for others a source of pride in Norwegian heritage. You don't have to be Norwegian to love Norwegian knitting, though; you just have to appreciate beauty, warmth, and a little bit of history.

In Selbu, near Trondheim, it was a tradition for the bride to give patterned mittens to all the members of her wedding party. Knitting was an expression of creativity and skill. Immigrants brought many of these skills, traditions, and textiles with them when they immigrated to the United States.

The design of embroidered church mittens and gloves varies by the Norwegian region in which they were made. The floral embroidery on mittens from Hallingdal, for example, is symmetrical and grows in layered petals from a tight bud. In contrast, the embroidery on gloves from Telemark is asymmetrical. Floral motifs are based on C- or S-shaped curves.

Two-color, stranded, or pattern-knit mittens and gloves have small patterns on the palm for durability and larger patterns on the backs of the hands. Eight-petal flowers, called *åttebladroser*, are common motifs. They look to us like snowflakes or stars. Animals, initials, and other floral motifs appear on the backs, thumbs, and cuffs. The cuffs, by the way, might be ribbed if the intended wearer were male, or lacy if the intended wearer were female.

Sheep shearing, Telemark, Norway, 1890s.
GAUSTA COLLECTION, VESTERHEIM ARCHIV

Gjermund Gaustad mending nets in a well-worn sweater, Tinn, Telemark, Norway, 1890s.
GAUSTA COLLECTION, VESTERHEIM ARCHIVE

Introduction

Norwegian knitting usually conjures up visions of ski sweaters worn by the Scandinavian teams at the Winter Olympics. It was the beauty and relative simplicity of these sweaters that inspired us to learn more about Norwegian fiber traditions. We were first introduced to Vesterheim Norwegian-American Museum through various fiber-related classes that they offered, including spinning, *nålbinding*, Setesdal embroidery, band weaving, bentwood box making, and felt making. Vesterheim is the oldest and most comprehensive museum in the United States dedicated to a single immigrant group, Norwegian Americans.

On a trip to the museum over Halloween weekend in 2004 for the band-weaving class, we were invited for a behind-the-scenes peek at the textile collection. The sheer magnitude of the collection was very impressive. We marveled at drawers filled with colorful mittens and gloves, racks loaded with incredible embroidered *bunads*, and rolls of exquisite tapestries. After picking our chins up off the floor, we turned to one another and announced together, "We need to create a book!"

We journeyed again to Vesterheim on Thanksgiving weekend and between squeals of childlike delight, we began the process of putting ideas to paper and needles; *Norwegian Handknits* was conceived.

Over the next few years, we took many trips to Vesterheim. During our drive to Decorah, we were

A view of Seed Savers.

always impressed by a sign for Seed Savers, an heirloom seed farm. This farm strives to ensure the preservation of old seeds by growing ancient plant varieties and selling the seeds to gardeners who in turn propagate them. If a seed is not planted in a few years, it will dry out and fail to germinate a new crop.

We immediately drew a parallel to our work designing new patterns from the textiles housed in the collection at Vesterheim. As knitters, we are the farmers, and the designs in this book are the seeds. We want to nurture these old fiber traditions to ensure they are not forgotten. With this book, we hope to help preserve the heritage of the Norwegian people who immigrated to their "western home."

As we studied the artifacts and reviewed old photos, we felt a connection to the knitter, weaver, painter, needleworker, or artist who made the piece. We imagined what it would have been like to live in the mountains of Norway or do the daily chores on a farm in a new land. The inspiration for some of the patterns came very naturally by just modifying the old design. Other patterns, such as the Voss Family Sweaters, took extensive study of the artifact and days of graphing various pattern possibilities. The end result is a collection of patterns steeped in Norwegian history that we hope you will enjoy knitting for family and friends.

Using Basic Knitting Techniques

Margit Gardsjord Kostveit and her daughter, Telemark, Norway, 1890s.
GAUSTA COLLECTION, VESTERHEIM ARCHIVE

The textiles at Vesterheim are examples of exceptional work stitched with loving hands. Many of the items were made for special occasions, such as weddings or holiday celebrations. There are very few daily-wear items found in the museum collection. It is believed that either not many daily-wear items survived, or the benefactors felt that the items were not worthy of donation. That said, we did discover a few basic utilitarian garments for everyday use; these garments, though simple, still demonstrated the skill and creativity of the creator. We chose to include a few of these easy-to-knit, yet elegant garments in this chapter. The need for warm, functional knitting was key to remaining comfortable while moving around the farm doing chores. Since homes relied on wood fireplaces to keep warm, a cozy garment or accessory was always welcome. In Ruth's collection, the basic knit and purl stitch are used to create a thicker fabric, which provided better insulation.

Ruth's Cap

Size
To fit newborn baby to toddler
Finished Measurement
Circumference: 14 ¾"

Materials

- Dale of Norway *Baby Ull*
  (100% superwash merino wool;
  180 yds/50g per ball)
  1 ball Soft Yellow #2203
- Size 2 (2.75mm) double-
  pointed needles (set of 5) and
  two 16" circular needles, or size
  needed to obtain gauge
- Small crochet hook
- Stitch markers, 1 in CC for beg
  of rnd
- Tapestry needle
- Pom-pom maker (optional)

Gauge
26 sts and 48 rnds = 4" (10cm) in
pat st.
*Adjust needle size as necessary to
obtain correct gauge.*

When we saw the original cap at the museum, we could almost picture the baby who wore it—full, red cheeks, a sweet temperament—this child was definitely the apple of his or her daddy's eye. We love the simplicity and beauty of this pattern—garter stitch columns paired with stockinette rows that are dotted with a garter ridge. The stitch pattern used in the cap lends itself to many items, so we've created Ruth's Collection.

We made a few changes when we knitted Ruth's Cap. The original was knit in rayon, but we used machine-washable wool produced just for a baby. We also added a firmer-fitting cuff and hidden decreases to bring the pattern all the way to the fluffy pom-pom on its crown.

The knit cap in Ruth's Collection was the inspiration for Ruth's Cap. It was made by Mina Elstad Quickstad for her daughter Ruth (b. Nov. 8, 1891) of Toronto, South Dakota.

Special Technique

Provisional Cast-On: With crochet hook and waste yarn, make a chain several sts longer than desired cast-on. With knitting needle and project yarn, pick up indicated number of sts in the "bumps" on back of chain. When indicated in pattern, "unzip" the crochet chain to free live sts.

Pattern Stitch

Multiple of 12 sts
Rnds 1 and 3: Knit.
Rnd 2: *P5, k1; rep from * around.
Rnd 4: *P5, k7; rep from * around.
Rep Rnds 1–4 for pat.

Pattern Note

Switch to double-pointed needles when stitches no longer fit comfortably on circular needle.

Instructions

HEM

Using provisional method and circular needle, CO 96 sts; pm for beg of rnd and join, taking care not to twist sts.
Knit 10 rnds.
Turning rnd: Purl.
Knit 10 rnds.
Unzip provisional cast-on, placing live sts on 2nd circular needle; fold hem at turning rnd so that needles are parallel.
Joining rnd: Using the needle in front, *insert right tip into first st on front needle, then into first st on back needle and knit them tog; rep from * around—96 sts.

BODY

Beg with Rnd 2 of chart, work even in pat st for 4 ½", ending with either Rnd 2 or 4; on last rnd, place markers every 6 sts around.

CROWN

Dec rnd: Maintaining est pat, *work to 2 sts before marker, k2tog, rep from * around—80 sts.
Next rnd: Work even.
Rep last 2 rnds twice more, working decs at vertical St st ridges—48 sts.
Next rnd: Removing markers, k2tog around—24 sts.
Next rnd: Work even.
Next rnd: K2tog around—12 sts.
Break yarn, leaving a 6" tail; thread through rem sts, pull tight, and secure tail to WS.

Finishing

Weave in all ends.

Block to finished measurements.

POM-POM

Use pom-pom maker or follow instructions as follows:
Cut 2 cardboard circles the size of desired pom-pom. Cut a hole in the center of each circle, approx ½" in diameter. Thread a tapestry needle with 1 very long strand each of all colors. Holding both circles together, insert needle through center hole, over the outside edge, through center again, going around and around until entire circle is covered and center hole is filled (thread more length of yarn as needed). With sharp scissors, cut yarn between the 2 circles all around the circumference. Using 2 [12"] strands of yarn (tying ends), wrap yarn between circles, going 2 or 3 times around; pull tight and tie into a firm knot. Remove cardboard and fluff out pom-pom. Trim ends as necessary to make pom-pom circular. Attach pom-pom to hat using tying ends.

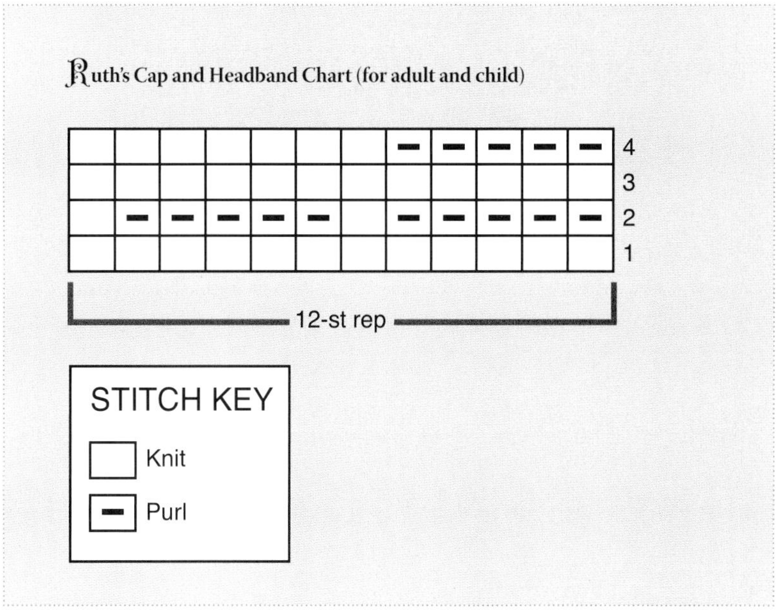

Ruth's Cap and Headband Chart (for adult and child)

12-st rep

STITCH KEY

Knit

Purl

Adult Ruth's Cap

Size
Adult average

Finished Measurements
Circumference: 22 ½"
Length: 9 ½"

Materials

- Dale of Norway *Free Style* (100% superwash wool; 87 yds/50g per ball): 2 balls Aubergine #5072
- Size 7 (4.5mm) double-pointed needles (set of 5) and two 16" circular needles or size needed to obtain gauge
- Medium-size crochet hook
- Stitch markers, 1 in CC for beg of rnd
- Tapestry needle

Gauge
17 sts and 24 rnds = 4" (10cm) in pat st.
Adjust needle size as necessary to obtain correct gauge.

If it's good enough for kids . . . Here is the "grown-up" version of this charming cap, with small touches of adult sophistication. This cap is perfect for those cold weekend mornings when we in the Midwest get reacquainted with our snowblowers.

Pattern Stitch
See chart on page 15.

Special Technique
Provisional Cast-On: With crochet hook and waste yarn, make a chain several sts longer than desired cast-on. With knitting needle and project yarn, pick up indicated number of sts in the "bumps" on back of chain. When indicated in pattern, "unzip" the crochet chain to free live sts.

Pattern Note
Switch to double-pointed needles when stitches no longer fit comfortably on circular needle.

Instructions

HEM

Using provisional method and circular needle, CO 96 sts; pm for beg of rnd and join, taking care not to twist sts.

Knit 10 rnds.

Turning rnd: Purl.

Knit 10 rnds.

Unzip provisional cast-on, placing live sts on 2nd circular needle; fold hem at turning rnd so that needles are parallel.

Joining rnd: Using the needle in front, *insert right tip into first st on front needle, then into first st on back needle and knit them tog; rep from * around—96 sts.

BODY

Beg with Rnd 2 of chart, work even in pat st for 6", ending with either Rnd 2 or 4; on last rnd, place markers every 6 sts around.

CROWN

Dec rnd: Maintaining est pat, *work to 2 sts before marker, k2tog, rep from * around—80 sts.

Next rnd: Work even.

Rep last 2 rnds twice more, working decs at vertical St st ridges—48 sts.

Next rnd: Removing markers, k2tog around—24 sts.

Next rnd: Work even.

Next rnd: K2tog around—12 sts.

Break yarn, leaving a 6" tail; thread through rem sts, pull tight, and secure tail to WS.

Finishing

Weave in all ends.

Block to finished measurements.

Make tassel and tail as desired; sew to top of cap.

OLD NORWEGIAN RECIPE

ALMOND RUSKS

THERE IS SOMETHING ABOUT THE SMELL OF ALMONDS BAKING THAT BRINGS BACK LOVING MEMORIES OF FAMILY GATHERINGS. IT'S HARD TO EXPLAIN, BUT IT ALWAYS MAKES ME SMILE.

2 EGGS

1 c. BROWN SUGAR

7 TBSP. SOFT BUTTER, CREAMED

3 TBSP. ALMONDS, SLIVERED

3 c. FLOUR

1 TSP. BAKING POWDER

DASH OF SALT

PREHEAT OVEN TO 375° F. BEAT EGGS AND SUGAR TOGETHER UNTIL LIGHT. ADD THE CREAMED BUTTER AND THE ALMONDS. SIFT DRY INGREDIENTS AND ADD A LITTLE AT A TIME TO BUTTER MIXTURE, BEATING WELL AFTER EACH ADDITION. SPREAD THE DOUGH 1½ INCHES THICK ON A LIGHTLY BUTTERED BAKING SHEET. BAKE FOR 15 MINUTES, UNTIL BROWN. REMOVE FROM BAKING SHEET AND CUT RUSKS DIAGONALLY INTO PIECES ¾ INCH THICK WHILE STILL WARM. COOL AND ENJOY.

A Visit with Enid Grindland

On a beautiful day during an unusually cold Minnesota spring, we set out for Lake Carlos, located just outside Alexandria, Minnesota, to meet Enid Grindland. We wanted to learn more about the women in her family, who had made a few of the items in the collection at Vesterheim that inspired some of our designs.

With no trouble at all, thanks in part to Enid's map, we found her charming home on Lake Carlos. She and her husband, Cliff, expanded the family summer cabin and now live there year-round. To our delight and amazement, we discovered that Enid is a champion *rosemaler*, an expert in the traditional Norwegian painting that embellishes trunks, chairs, cupboards, bowls, plates, and almost anything else paint will adhere to.

After some introductions and a tour of their home, Enid introduced us to her family through photographs, stories, and one particular family treasure, a handwritten diary or daybook kept by Enid's mother, Ruth Quickstad Jerde. In the book, Ruth includes a history of her family and other personal recollections.

As a baby, Ruth wore the hat that was the inspiration for the Ruth's Cap pattern. The original hat was made by Ruth's mother, Mina Elstad Quickstad (1871–1924). Mina had a lifelong love of music and was always disappointed that she was never able to study it formally.

We spent the afternoon sharing many family stories, experiences, and—as is always the case in a good Norwegian home—a cup of coffee and sweets. We left Enid and Cliff as if we were old friends, with an open invitation to come back again sometime soon.

Cliff and Enid Grindland in their Alexandria, Minnesota home. Examples of Enid's rosemaling are displayed on the wall behind them.

Enid, center, with her family, father Edward Jerde, mother Ruth Jerde, and brothers Randolph, Desmond, and Waldo.

Ruth's Mittens

These mittens are a natural choice for the garter stitch pattern. The garter stitch has a wonderful stretch for a warm, snug, but not tight-fitting mitten. Knit in the spring green Free Style yarn, the mittens bring a promise of new life through the long winter months. Add the ruffle for your favorite snow bunny, or skip the ruffle if you are knitting for your favorite ski bum.

Special Abbreviations

M1L (Make 1 Left): Insert LH needle from front to back under the running thread between the last st worked and next st on LH needle; knit into the back of resulting loop.

M1R (Make 1 Right): Insert LH needle from back to front under the running thread between the last st worked and next st on LH needle; knit into the front of resulting loop.

N1, N2, N3, N4: Needles 1, 2, 3, 4

Instructions

RIGHT MITTEN

Ruffled Cuff

With smaller needles, CO 68 sts and distribute on 4 dpns; pm for beg of rnd and join, taking care not to twist sts.

Knit 2 rnds.

Dec rnd: K2tog around—34 sts.

Work 14 rnds in K1, p1 Rib.

Thumb Gusset

Change to larger needles.

Work Rnd 1 of chart and inc 2 sts evenly around—36 sts.

Work 4 rnds even following chart, and on last rnd, pm after first st for thumb gusset.

Inc rnd: M1R, knit to marker, M1L, slip marker, work in est pat around—38 sts.

Next rnd: Work even, working St st between beg of rnd and thumb gusset markers and maintaining pat on all other sts.

Rep [last 2 rnds] 7 times, then rep Inc rnd once more—54 sts, with 19 sts in thumb gusset section.

Next rnd: Slip 19 thumb gusset sts to waste yarn, CO 1 above opening, work in est pat around—36 sts.

Main Mitten

Rearrange sts so that there are 9 sts on each of the 4 dpns.

Work even in est pat for 3" (or 2" short of desired finished length), ending with Rnd 3 or 4.

Size

Adult average

Finished Measurements

Circumference (around hand): 8"
Length: 9"

Materials

- Dale of Norway *Free Style* (100% superwash wool; 87 yds/50g per ball): 2 balls Spring Green #9133
- Size 5 (3.75mm) double-pointed needles (set of 5)
- Size 7 (4.5mm) double-pointed needles (set of 5) or size needed to obtain gauge
- Stitch markers, 1 in CC for beg of rnd
- Tapestry needle

Gauge

17 sts and 24 rnds = 4" (10cm) in pat st with larger needles.
Adjust needle size as necessary to obtain correct gauge.

Top Decrease

Dec rnd: N1: K1, ssk, work in pat to end; N2: work in pat to last 3 sts, k2tog, k1; N3 and N4: work as for N1 and N2—32 sts.

Next rnd: Work even in est pat.

Rep [last 2 rnds] 4 more times—16 sts.

Break yarn, leaving a 6" tail; thread tail through rem sts, pull tight, and secure tail to WS.

Thumb

Slip the 19 sts from waste yarn to 3 larger dpns.

Rnd 1: Beg at 1-st CO, pick up and knit 1 st, knit to end, then pick up and knit 1 st—21 sts.

Rnd 2: K2tog, knit to last 2 sts, k2tog—19 sts.

Work even for 8 rnds or until thumb section reaches beg of your thumbnail.

Dec rnd: K1, *k2tog, k1; rep from * around—13 sts.

Next rnd 2: Knit.

Rep last 2 rnds once more—9 sts.

Next rnd: [K2tog, k1] 3 times—3 sts.

Break yarn, leaving a 6" tail; thread tail through rem sts, pull tight, and secure tail to WS.

LEFT MITTEN

Work as for Right Mitten to Inc rnd for thumb gusset, but on last rnd, place markers following 18th and 19th sts for thumb gusset.

Inc rnd: Work in est pat to first marker, slip marker, M1R, knit to 2nd marker, M1L, slip marker, work in est pat to end of rnd—38 sts.

Next rnd: Work even, working St st between thumb gusset markers and maintaining pat on all other sts.

Rep [last 2 rnds] 7 times, then rep Inc rnd once more—54 sts, with 19 sts in thumb gusset section.

Next rnd: Work in est pat to marker, slip 19 thumb gusset sts to waste yarn, CO 1 above opening, work in est pat around—36 sts. Cont as for Right Mitten.

Finishing

Weave in all ends. Block as necessary.

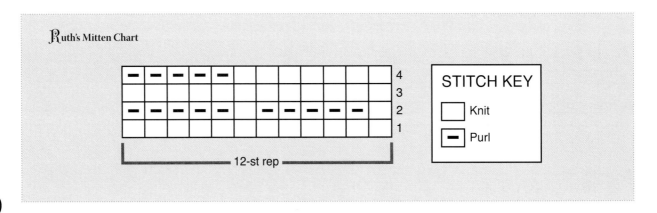

Ruth's Mitten Chart

12-st rep

STITCH KEY

☐ Knit

⊟ Purl

Ruth's Headband

We think of this headband as a sampler, a beginner's project with a lot of technique for the new knitter who's wondering what to make after all those scarves. This fast and easy headband introduces the concepts of reading a chart and working on circular needles. The experienced knitter will appreciate the garter pattern for its give and simple good looks.

Pattern Stitch
Multiple of 12 sts
Rnds 1 and 3: Knit.
Rnd 2: *P5, k1; rep from * around.
Rnd 4: *P5, k7; rep from * around.
Rep Rnds 1–4 for pat.

Special Technique
Provisional Cast-On: With crochet hook and waste yarn, make a chain several sts longer than desired cast-on. With knitting needle and project yarn, pick up indicated number of sts in the "bumps" on back of chain. When indicated in pattern, "unzip" the crochet chain to free live sts.

HEM
Using provisional method, CO 96 sts; pm for beg of rnd and join, taking care not to twist sts.
Knit 5 rnds.
Turning rnd: Purl.
Knit 5 rnds.
Unzip provisional cast-on, placing live sts on 2nd circular needle; fold work along turning rnd so that are needles parallel.
Joining rnd: Using the needle in front, *insert the right tip into the first st on the front needle, then into the first st on the back needle and knit them tog; rep from * around—96 sts.

BODY
Work 10 rnds in pat following text or chart (see page 15).

HEM
Knit 5 rnds.
Turning rnd: Purl.
Knit 5 rnds, leaving sts on needle after last rnd.
Break yarn, leaving a very long tail.
Turn in hem on turning rnd and loosely sew live sts to inside of headband.

Finishing
Block to finished measurements.

Size
Adult average

Finished Measurements
Circumference: 22 ½"
Width: 3 ½"

Materials

- Dale of Norway *Free Style* (100% superwash wool; 87 yds/50g per ball): 1 ball Rust #3946
- 2 size 7 (4.5mm) 16" circular needles or size needed to obtain gauge
- Medium-size crochet hook
- Tapestry needle

Gauge
17 sts and 24 rnds = 4" (10cm) in pat st.
Adjust needle size as necessary to obtain correct gauge.

Ruth's Baby Blanket

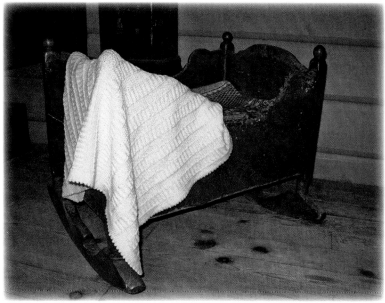

Finished Measurements
Approx. 32" x 36"

Materials

- Dale of Norway *Baby Ull* (100% superwash merino wool; 180 yds/50g per ball): 9 balls Soft Yellow #2203
- Size 3 (3.25mm) 40" circular needle or 1 size smaller than body of blanket
- Size 4 (3.5mm) 36" circular needle or size needed to obtain gauge
- Stitch markers, 1 in CC for beg of rnd
- Tapestry needle

Gauge
24 sts and 36 rows = 4" (10cm) in pat st with larger needle.
Adjust needle size as necessary to obtain correct gauge.

This pattern is so soothing to knit. To make a larger afghan, simply figure out your stitch gauge, multiply your desired width by the stitch gauge, and adjust it to be a multiple of 12 stitches and 9 "balancing" stitches. Cast on this number of stitches and knit until the afghan is as long as you want it to be.

Pattern Stitch
See Baby Ruth Chart .
Multiple of 12 sts + 9.
Rows 1 and 3 (RS): Knit.
Row 2: K1, *p1, k5; rep from * to last 2 sts, p1, k1.
Row 4: K1, p1, k5, *p7, k5; rep from * to last 2 sts, p1, k1.
Rep Rows 1–4 for pat.

Special Technique
Provisional Cast-On: With crochet hook and waste yarn, make a chain several sts longer than desired cast-on. With knitting needle and project yarn, pick up indicated number of sts in the "bumps" on back of chain. When indicated in pattern, "unzip" the crochet chain to free live sts.

Pattern Note
The border and facing are worked around the main blanket with shaping increases and decreases worked in the corners.

Instructions

MAIN BLANKET

Using provisional method and larger needle, CO 177 sts.
Beg with Row 2, work even in pat until piece measures 34", ending with a RS row; leave sts on needle.

BORDER AND FACING

With RS facing and using smaller needle, pick up and knit 3 sts for every 4 rows along left edge, making sure that you have an even number of sts, pm; unzip provisional CO and slip live sts to needle; pick up and knit 3 sts for every 4 rows along right edge, making sure that you have an even number of sts, pm; knit across top sts, pm for beg of rnd.

Rnd 1: *K1, M1L, knit to next marker, M1R, slip marker; rep from * around (see page 19).

Rnd 2: Knit.

Rnd 3–8: Rep Rnds 1 and 2.

Rnd 9: Purl.

Rnd 10: *K1, k2tog, knit to 2 sts before marker, ssk, slip marker; rep from * around.

Rnd 11: Knit.

Rnds 12–17: Rep Rnds 1 and 2.

Loosely BO all sts, making sure that the side bind-off sts are very loose and stretchy.

Finishing

Sew edge of border facing to WS, making sure that it remains elastic.
Weave in all ends.
Block as necessary.

Julia Rosendahl Peterson (left) and daughter Gena (right) on an outing, early 1900s. ROSENDAHL COLLECTION, VESTERHEIM ARCHIVE

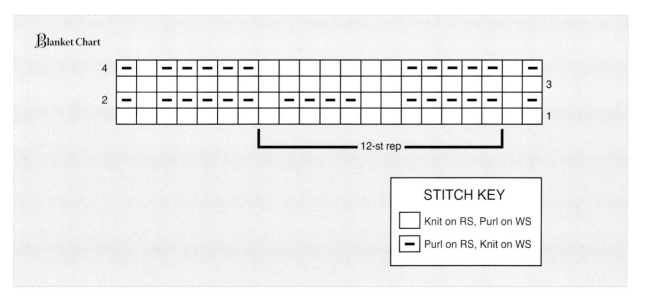

𝔅lanket Chart

12-st rep

STITCH KEY

☐ Knit on RS, Purl on WS

▬ Purl on RS, Knit on WS

OLD NORWEGIAN RECIPE

ROMMEGROT

(NORWEGIAN CREAM PORRIDGE)

ROMMEGROT IS A CREAM PORRIDGE THAT IS SERVED ON SPECIAL OCCASIONS. THE CONTROVERSY THAT SURROUNDS THE ELVES' FAVORITE DISH IS IF IT SHOULD BE MADE WITH SWEET OR SOUR CREAM. TRADITIONAL *ROMMEGROT* IS MADE WITH SOUR CREAM, WHICH IS THE WAY I LEARNED TO MAKE IT. HOWEVER, IT IS NOT UNCOMMON TO FIND RECIPES THAT USE SWEET CREAM INSTEAD. WHICHEVER CREAM YOU CHOOSE, THE RESULT IS A WONDERFULLY CREAMY TREAT.

    2 c. SOUR CREAM
    1 c. FLOUR
    1 ½ c. HOT MILK
    ½ TSP. SALT
    2 TBSP. + ½ c. SUGAR, DIVIDED
    ½ TBSP. CINNAMON

PUT SOUR CREAM IN KETTLE AND BRING TO A BOIL. ADD ENOUGH FLOUR TO MAKE A THICK MUSH (ABOUT ½ CUP FOR EACH CUP OF CREAM), AND REDUCE HEAT TO A SLOW SIMMER, STIRRING CONTINUOUSLY WITH AN OLD-FASHIONED WHISK. REMOVE ANY BUTTER THAT RISES TO THE SURFACE WITH A SPOON AND SET IT ASIDE. ADD ENOUGH HOT MILK TO OBTAIN A PORRIDGE-LIKE CONSISTENCY, AND CONTINUE STIRRING UNTIL NO MORE BUTTER RISES, ABOUT 15 TO 20 MINUTES. ADD 2 TBSP. SUGAR AND MORE FLOUR TO MAKE A THICK MUSH. BEAT WELL. IN A SMALL BOWL, COMBINE REMAINING ½ c. SUGAR WITH CINNAMON. SERVE PORRIDGE HOT WITH MELTED BUTTER (FROM CREAM) AND SPRINKLE WITH CINNAMON SUGAR.

Nisse History

"The Elves" tapestry.   LUTHER COLLEGE COLLECTION

A Nisse is a Norwegian folklore elf who is recognized by his red stocking cap. In a tapestry weaving by Pauline Fjelde, two Nisse are taunted by a magpie that has stolen their spoon. The Nisse will guard the family farm as long as they are provided with bowls of porridge and will resort to mischief if the porridge is not provided. The magpie is teasing the Nisse because, without the spoon, the "little dickens" will not be able to enjoy the nice warm bowl of porridge.

The Nisse character has childlike appeal and is mentioned in many a Norwegian folk song and folklore. When Hitler's troops occupied Norway during World War II, some Norwegians wore a Nisse-style red stocking cap as a sign of defiance. Illustrations of the Nisse, which were normally used on Christmas cards, along with depictions of the Norwegian flag, were banned during the Nazi occupation.

Pauline Fjelde wove *The Elves* tapestry in 1892 in Minneapolis, Minnesota. Pauline (1861–1923) was born in Ålesund, Norway, and immigrated to Minneapolis in 1887. Pauline was also well known for her embroidery; she and her sister, Thomane, embroidered the first Minnesota state flag.

Nisse Hats

A tapestry weaving by Pauline Fjelde from the original Luther College Collection provided inspiration for the Nisse Hats. The hat can be made for a child, for the child's favorite stuffed animal or for an egg. (Norwegians love eggs for breakfast!). Watch out, you may find some little tricks played on you by your own little Nisse.

Pattern Note

For Child's hat, begin with circular needle, then change to double-pointed needles when stitches no longer fit comfortably on the circular needle; for smaller-size hats, use double-pointed needles throughout.

Instructions

CO 136 (64, 48) sts; pm for beg of rnd and join, being careful not to twist sts.

Work even in St st (knit all rnds) until piece measures 6 (2, 1)".

Next rnd: *K17 (8, 6), pm; rep from * around.

Dec rnd: *Knit to 2 sts before marker, k2tog; rep from * around—128 (56, 40) sts rem.

Knit 4 rnds even.

Rep [last 5 rnds] 14 (5, 3) times—16 sts.

Next rnd: K2tog around—8 sts.

Knit 2 rnds.

Break yarn, leaving a 6" tail; using tapestry needle, thread tail through rem sts, pull tight, and secure.

Finishing

Weave in all ends. Block to finished measurements.

Sizes

Child (Teddy bear, Egg)
Instructions are written for largest size with smaller sizes in parentheses. When only 1 number is given, it applies to all sizes.

Finished Measurement

Circumference: 17 (8, 6)"

Materials

- Dale of Norway *Baby Ull* (100% superwash merino wool; 180 yds/50g per skein): 2 (1, 1) skein(s) Red #4018
- Size 2 (2.75mm) 16" circular and/or double-pointed needles (set of 5) or size needed to obtain gauge
- Stitch markers, 1 in CC for beg of rnd
- Tapestry needle

Gauge

32 sts and 44 rnds = 4" (10cm) in St st.
Adjust needle size as necessary to obtain correct gauge.

Traditional Norwegian Folk Song

The Nisse in the barn has got his Christmas treat, so good and sweet, so good and sweet.

He nods his head and smiles, oh so happily, 'cause Christmas pudding he just loves to eat!

And around him stand the rats that think he's sharing, and they're staring, and they're staring.

They are also very fond of Christmas pudding, and they're dancing, dancing in a ring!

Work Day Shawl

Finished Measurements
Approx. 38" x 44"
(including border)

Materials

- Version 1: Blackberry Ridge *Traditional Colors 100% Wool, Medium Weight* (100% wool; 250 yds/4 oz per skein): 4 skeins Medium Chestnut
- Version 2: Raumagarn *Strikkegarn* (100% wool; 115 yds/50g per skein), 9 skeins Medium Gray #113
- Size 10 (6mm) 29" circular needles or size needed to obtain gauge
- Size 6 (4mm) double-pointed needles (2), or 4 sizes smaller than needle used for center of shawl
- Cotton waste yarn
- Tapestry needle
- Stitch markers

Gauge
16 sts and 32 rows = 4" (10cm) in garter st with larger needles, blocked.
Achieving gauge is not critical for this project; the center of the shawl should be a loose gauge and the border, a tighter gauge.

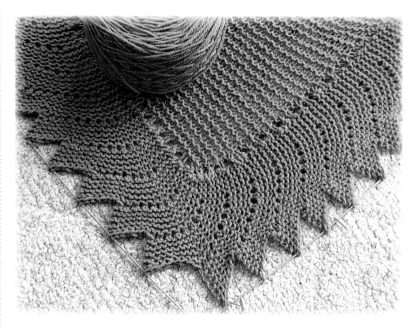

We were inspired by this shawl's simplicity and hearty wearability. We envision a Norwegian woman wearing it on a homestead on the Midwestern plains. This immigrant woman worked hard for her land, for her family, and for her legacy of a better life in America. We knit our shawl out of Blackberry Ridge wool and Raumagarn *Strikkegarn*, yarns that are hearty but still comforting. Make yours with the same yarn or of cashmere; whatever the fiber, the shawl will keep you wrapped in the legacy promised by our foremother.

Special Technique
Provisional Cast-On: With crochet hook and waste yarn, make a chain several sts longer than desired cast-on. With knitting needle and project yarn, pick up indicated number of sts in the "bumps" on back of chain. When indicated in pattern, "unzip" the crochet chain to free live sts.

Pattern Note
This shawl is worked in two parts: the center and the border. The center is simple garter stitch worked on large needles, which is then surrounded by a round of eyelets. The border is an easy garter-based eyelet sawtooth, worked perpendicularly to the center stitches and attached to the eyelet round by working an ssk decrease on every right-side row, joining the last border stitch with the next eyelet round stitch. When rounding the corners, the edging is eased around by working the ssk every other right-side row.

Instructions

CENTER

With circular needle and using provisional method, CO 120 sts. Mark RS of work.

Knit 288 rows (144 garter ridges) ending with a WS row; do not break yarn.

Place sts on long length of cotton waste yarn and block, stretching as much as you can; you should see an open, holey fabric.

Slip sts back to circular needle.

LACE EDGE

Pickup row: Pick up (without knitting) 1 st for every garter ridge along right edge; unzip provisional cast-on and put live sts on needle; pick up (without knitting) 1 st for every garter ridge along left edge—528 sts.

Eyelet rnd (RS): *K1, yo, k2tog, yo; rep from * around, and *at the same time*, mark off 12-st corner sections by placing markers after first 6 sts of each side and before last 6 sts of each side. Break yarn, leaving a 6" tail.

Slip first 6 sts of rnd (corner sts) to RH needle tip for new beg of rnd.

SAWTOOTH BORDER

Using provisional method and smaller dpn, CO 20 sts.

Rows 1, 3, 5, 7, 9 (RS): K19, ssk last st tog with first st on circular needle; turn.

Row 2 and all WS rows: K20, turn.

Row 11: BO 8 sts (1 st rem on needle), [yo, k1] 7 times, yo, k3, ssk; turn.

Row 12: K20, turn.

Rep Rows 1–12 to first corner marker.

CORNER SECTION

Rows 1, 2, 4, 5, 6, 8, 9, 10: K20; turn.

Rows 3 and 7: K19, ssk; turn.

Row 11: BO 8 sts (1 st rem on needle), [yo, k1] 7 times, yo, k3, ssk; turn.

Row 12: K20; turn.

Rep [Corner Rows 1–12] 3 more times to next corner marker, attaching border on every other RS row.

*Work Sawtooth Border along left edge to next corner marker; work Corner Rows between corner markers; rep from * along bottom and right edges, ending with top right corner sts.

Unzip provisional cast-on and slip live sts to dpn. Join border ends by working Kitchener st in garter.

Finishing

Weave in ends.

Block entire shawl.

Above: This shawl belonged to Henriette Naeseth (1899–1987), a professor of English at Augustana College in Rock Island, Illinois, or her aunt, Marie Koren (1874–1968), longtime organist at Washington Prairie Lutheran Church, Decorah, Iowa.

Below: Work Day Shawl in gray.

Simple Knitting With Embellishments

The decorative aspect of Norwegian knitting, without the use of two-color knitting, is highlighted in this chapter. We discovered many items in the collection that were created using plain knitting and then embellished with surface decoration. In this chapter, we've included projects that feature older techniques such as felting, embroidery, and pile shag along with a few projects that include more modern embellishment techniques like needle felting and beaded knitting.

Bread Drawer Scarf with Felted Bobbles

At Vesterheim, smaller pieces are stored in an ingenious way—on a rack that looks very much like a bread-proofing rack, with cookie sheets and baking pans as drawers. The lace items in the collection are stored here. The small lace sampler that inspired the pattern in the scarf was the final item we found at the very bottom of the last drawer.

The basic pattern incorporates four stitches of garter between six stitches of yarn-over lace. It is a nice pattern for a beginner knitter who is interested in trying lace.

The felted bobbles used on the tassels dip into the Nordic tradition of felt making. Kate Martinson, fiber artist and professor at Luther College in Decorah, Iowa, provided the directions for felting the bobbles.

Finished Measurements
9" x 80" (excluding fringe)

Materials

- Reynolds *Soft Sea Wool* (100% wool; 162yds/50g per skein): 5 skeins Light Blue #0514
- Size 4 (3.5mm) needles or size needed to obtain gauge
- Medium-size crochet hook
- Embroidery needle
- DMC floss (8.7 yds/hank): 1 hank Light Blue #3841
- Tapestry needle (small enough to fit through bead hole)
- Sharp tapestry needle
- 36 crystal beads size (11/0)
- Materials for felted balls (see sidebar p. 31)

Gauge
22 sts and 44 rows = 4" (10cm) in lace pat.
Adjust needle size as necessary to obtain gauge.

This lace sampler (doily, washcloth) was made by Bertha Hagen Wickney of Northwood, North Dakota. Bertha was born in 1854 in Brandbu, Hadeland, Norway. She immigrated with her family in 1860 or 1861 to Allamakee County, Iowa. She married Andrew Wickney in 1879 and settled near Northwood, North Dakota. She died in 1899.

Instructions

SCARF

CO 48 sts.

Knit 8 rows.

Work lace pat as follows:

Row 1 and all WS rows: K6, [p6, k4] 3 times, p6, k6.

Row 2: K7, [yo, ssk, k8] 3 times, yo, ssk, k9.

Row 4: [K8, yo, ssk] 4 times, k8.

Row 6: K9, [yo, ssk, k8] 3 times, yo, ssk, k7.

Row 8: K10, [yo, ssk, k8] 3 times, yo, ssk, k6.

Rep Rows 1–8 of lace pat until scarf measures 79".

Knit 8 rows.

Bind off.

Block to finished measurements.

FELTED BALLS

(make 18)

Measure off 18 strands of yarn, 4 yds each. Follow directions in sidebar for making each yarn strand into a felted ball.

FRINGE

Place 9 markers evenly spaced along cast-on and bound-off edges of scarf; you will attach fringe at these markers.

Cut 108 [12"] lengths of yarn. Bundle strands together in sets of 6 each. Attach fringe using a lark's-head knot as follows: Insert crochet hook through edge of scarf at marked position; fold strands in half over crochet hook and pull loop through edge of scarf, about 1"; insert strand ends through loop and pull to secure fringe. Thread all yarn from each set of fringe onto a sharp tapestry needle and thread through felted ball. Separate strands into sets of 3 and tie each set just underneath the felted ball.

EMBROIDERY

Split floss into 3 strands. Use the lazy-daisy stitch to make a flower on each side of the felted ball. With small tapestry needle and one strand of floss, sew a bead to the center of each flower.

Making Decorative Felt Balls

by Kate Martinson

Felt balls reflect the traditional dimensional felt work, or *toving*, practiced in Norway for the manufacture of books, mittens, and other sorts of outerwear. It was and remains a way to bypass the spinning of wool and subsequent manipulation of that yarn into the desired object. Instead of the object being held together by looping, weaving, etc., the object is formed as microscopic scales on each hair catch on one another.

Making simple felted balls can provide one with a broader knowledge of fiber structure. They are very useful as decorative accents, such as buttons, fringe, or tassels, on almost any textile.

ALKALINE WATER MIXTURE

2 c.   hot water

½ tsp.   ammonia

1 ½ tsp.   water softener (if water is hard)

Add a small portion of the bar of Fels Naptha to this hot, alkaline mixture and let stand for a few minutes. Solution should look slightly cloudy.

Materials

- Layers of wool—carded fleece, carded batt, roving, or yarn (if using wool yarn, take special notice of note below)
- Hot water
- Ammonia
- Water softener
- Fels Naphtha soap or other plain, hard-milled, or firm handmade soap
- Dry work surface/towels for hands
- Glass, sturdy plastic, or ceramic container
- Microwave to heat and reheat solution

(*Note:* No superwash wool should be used, and blends must be tried by making a sample. Animal fibers felt differently, and the addition of nonanimal fibers can retard or prevent good felting. If using prespun yarn, you must pay particular attention to the spin and ply of the yarn. The yarn must be sufficiently loose for the scales on hairs of neighboring yarns to catch. Tight spinning and plying will impact this bonding from strand to strand.)

Decorative felt balls adorn the Sami Mittens.

A few of the materials needed to make felt balls.

Photo 1

Photo 2

Photo 3

Photo 4

Photo 5

Procedure with Raw Wool

Step 1: Use hand-carded wool, a batt, or well-opened roving or top. Take a small sheet or portion of fiber and place on flat surface. Shape into rectangle and orient it in a long, horizontal position. Imagine that you are to wrap a parcel with this wool sheet. Begin by pretending that the parcel is in the center of the sheet. Bring up approximately one-third of the sheet on the horizontal edge and gently fold it over on itself. Repeat this process with the top third, bringing it over the other two layers. Roll the strip from one end toward the other. As you approach the end, begin to wrap the exposed fibers at the end over and around the entire roll in order to cover up the jellyroll-like sides and create a more even bundle. Wool [Photos 1, 2, and 3]

Go to Step 2 below.

Procedure with 2–3 Yards of Open, Lightly Plied, Non-superwash Wool Yarn

Step 1: Gather the yarn randomly into a bundle in the hand. Do not wrap into a ball, but gently fold and squish into a small wad in the hand. Set aside and proceed with Step 2. If you work with yarn, it is very important to do practice balls to be certain the yarn you are using will bind into a strong mass and that the size is correct for the application. Since balls made with yarn are best done in one step, it is important to have sufficient yarn in your hand when you start. Yarn [Photo 4]

Step 2: Place your empty hands in the hot water solution, remove the bar of soap, and rub your hands with the soap. Place the wool roll in the palm of one hand and submerge it in the hot water. (The soap prevents wool from sticking to your skin.) Keep your fist loose as you begin to flex it slightly; this will move the solution into the wool and under the wool scales, thereby gradually hardening the wool. Moving your hands slowly, make fifteen or twenty "squish" motions. Lift your hand out of the water. [Photos 5 and 6]

Step 3: When the entire piece has been moistened and hardened, rub the ball gently with circular motions of the hands. (This process is known as fulling, and it causes individual scales to entangle with other scales.) Place the ball in the center of one soapy upturned palm and cover it with your other well-soaped palm, keeping it slightly cupped. Begin with light circular motions of the entire top hand—imagine that your hands are forming peanut butter or sugar cookies. Keep your hands cupped enough for easy rotation. Periodically "refresh" the ball by plunging it into the hot water solution; gradually increase the pressure on the ball and the size of the circular motions and, at the same time, decrease the cupping of your hand. [Photos 7 and 8]

Step 4: Since the wool will hold together as it is pinched and pulled, increase the tension of your hands until the ball is firm; if you are using unspun fiber, add an additional layer of wool. (If using yarn, proceed to rinse ball as described in Step 7 below.) First place the firm ball onto your work surface and dry your hands completely. Wet wool will not stick to wet wool, so always use dry hands when handling dry wool. Place a new layer of fiber on your work surface, then wrap it around the ball that you've been fulling (see Step 1). [Photos 9 and 10]

Step 5: Repeat Steps 1–3 until the ball is the size that you want and is smooth and firm. You may change the colors of wool that you are using for each layer.

Step 6: If the ball develops a "flap" during the fulling, you may fix it by putting the ball down, drying your hands, and selecting a small sheet of the same wool. Place this dry patch on the problem area, moisten and soap your hands, and reharden the ball (Step 2). Be careful not to lift your fingers too far, or the patch may become dislodged. Continue through Steps 1–3. *Note:* If you are using yarn, you will not be able to fix flaps very easily. You should make another ball, embroider over the flap, or sew it into place at that point in order to reinforce the ball and hide the imperfections.

Step 7: Rinse. This is more challenging than you think! It is difficult to get the solution out of the microscopically bonded wool. Using a small bowl of fresh water, squeeze or flush water through the ball. Change the water repeatedly until the smell of the chemicals becomes less perceptible. The addition of a small amount of water softener into the solution can be a great help.

Step 8: Dry on a flat and open surface so air can circulate.

Photo 6

Photo 7

Photo 8

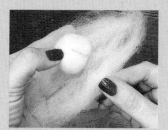

Photo 9

Photo 10

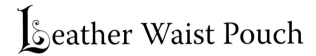

Leather Waist Pouch

The collection houses a number of examples of leather waist pouches. The waist pouch was commonly used by men and is considered a remnant of the Middle Ages, when garments did not have pockets. This knit version of a leather waist pouch can be made as a small bag with a shoulder strap or with belt loops to be worn at the waist. The embroidered version is inspired by the *bunad* collection.

Finished Measurements
6" x 7" (excluding strap)

Materials

- Cascade *220* (100% wool; 220yds/100g per skein): 1 skein Rust Heather #2435
- Size 10 ½ (6.5mm) double-pointed needles (set of 5) and 16" circular needles or size needed to obtain gauge
- Tapestry needle
- Stitch markers (1 in CC for beg of rnd)
- ¾" pewter button or felted-ball button
- Paternayan yarn from JCA for embroidery, 100% Persian Wool, 8 yd. skein, 8–10 various colors

Pre-fulled Gauge
15 sts and 20 rnds = 4" (10cm) in St st with single strand of yarn. *Gauge is not critical for this project; make sure that your sts are loose and airy.*

Special Technique
Fulling: Fulling is the process of shrinking an already-formed fabric by applying moisture, heat, and agitation. For knitted objects, this process is best done in a washing machine set on the hot, heavy-duty, ultra-clean cycle. Add ¼ cup fabric softener and 1 tablespoon vinegar to help the fiber scales open, then close, locking them together. Putting a pair of jeans or a tennis ball into the machine will help increase the agitation. For best results, run the item through the wash cycle only, checking the progress periodically. Allowing the object to go through the spin cycle may put creases in the fabric that can be hard to remove later. Some yarns and colors will need to go through the wash cycle twice or more. When the object has reached the desired size, remove from the machine, rinse in lukewarm water, shape as necessary, and allow to dry thoroughly.

Pattern Notes

- The pouch is worked in the round from top to bottom; change to double-pointed needles when stitches no longer fit comfortably on circular needle.
- The pouch flap is worked back and forth.
- Embroidery is done after fulling to finished size.

Instructions

POUCH

With single strand, CO 48 sts onto circular needle, pm for beg of rnd and join, taking care not to twist sts.

Rnd 1: K24, pm, k24.

Rnds 2–5: Knit.

Rnd 6: *Slip marker, k1, M1, knit to 1 st before marker, M1, k1, rep from * around—52 sts.

Rnds 7–8: Knit.

Rnds 9–23: Rep [Rnds 6–8] 5 times—72 sts.

Rnds 24–31: Knit.

Rnd 32: *Slip marker, k1, ssk, knit to 3 sts before marker, k2tog, k1, rep from * around—68 sts.

Rnd 33: Knit.

Rep [Rnds 32 and 33] 15 times—8 sts.

Break yarn; using tapestry needle, thread tail through rem sts, pull tight, and secure end.

FLAP

With RS facing, pick up and knit 24 sts along back of cast-on edge.

Row 1 (WS): K2, purl to last 2 sts, k2.

Row 2: Knit.

Rows 3 and 5: K2, purl to last 2 sts, k2.

Row 4: K2, M1, knit to last 2 sts, M1, k2—26 sts.

Row 6: Knit.

Row 7: K2, M1, purl to last 2 sts, M1, k2—28 sts.

Row 8: Knit.

Rows 9–14: Rep Rows 3–8—32 sts.

Row 15: K2, purl to last 2 sts, k2.

Row 16: K2, ssk, knit to last 4 sts, k2tog, k2—30 sts.

Rep [Rows 15 and 16] 8 times—14 sts.

Rep Row 15 once more.

Buttonhole Row: K2, ssk, k1, k2tog, [yo] twice, ssk, k1, k2tog, k2—12 sts.

Knitting in front and back of double yo on next row, rep [Rows 16 and 15] 3 times—6 sts.

BO and secure end of yarn.

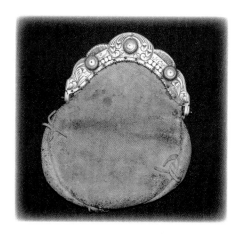

Leather purse/pouch, Norwegian. "Siwert Hoel" (a man's name—presumably the maker or owner) and "1795" (the date it was presumably made) are engraved on the clasp.

Close up of embroidered purse.

OPTION 1: I-CORD PURSE STRAP

With dpns, CO 5 sts.

Row 1: K5; do not turn; slide sts to opposite end of needle.

Rep Row 1 until I-cord measures 78".

BO and secure end of yarn.

Sew ends to sides of purse.

OPTION 2: I-CORD BELT BAG STRAPS (make 2)

With dpns, CO 5 sts.

Row 1: K5; do not turn; slide sts to opposite end of needle.

Rep Row 1 until I-cord measures 4".

BO and secure end of yarn.

Sew one end to top edge of back and other end to middle of back.

Weave in all ends.

Finishing

Full purse until it reaches finished measurements or desired size.

EMBROIDERY

When purse is completely dry, embroider as follows: Work solid sections in satin stitch, following the template. Use stem stitch or backstitch to outline solid sections once they have been competed. Sew button on bag opposite buttonhole.

Optional: Instead of button, make a felted ball (see page 31) and sew on opposite buttonhole.

Embroidery Template

﷽essenger Bag

A much roomier version of the leather waist pouch is created by increasing the number of stitches and rows, yet maintaining the same shaping used in the waist pouch.

Special Technique

Fulling: Fulling is the process of shrinking an already-formed fabric by applying moisture, heat, and agitation. For knitted objects, this process is best done in a washing machine set on the hot, heavy-duty, ultra-clean cycle. Add ¼ cup fabric softener and 1 tablespoon vinegar to help the fiber scales open, then close, locking them together. Putting a pair of jeans or a tennis ball into the machine will help increase the agitation. For best results, run the item through the wash cycle only, checking the progress periodically. Allowing the object to go through the spin cycle may put creases in the fabric that can be hard to remove later. Some yarns and colors will need to go through the wash cycle twice or more. When the object has reached the desired size, remove from the machine, rinse in lukewarm water, shape as necessary, and allow to dry thoroughly.

Pattern Notes

- The main bag is worked in the round from top to bottom; change to double-pointed needles when stitches no longer fit comfortably on circular needle.
- The bag flap is worked back and forth.
- After bag and strap are knit, they are fulled separately in washing machine.

Instructions

MAIN BAG

With single strand of yarn, CO 62 sts, pm, CO 62 sts; pm for beg of rnd and join, taking care not to twist sts—124 sts.

Knit 12 rnds.

Inc rnd: *K3, M1, knit to 3 sts before marker, M1, k3; rep from * once—128 sts.

Cont in St st and rep Inc rnd [every 3 rnds] 15 times, ending with an Inc rnd—188 sts.

Knit 20 rnds.

Dec rnd: *K3, ssk, knit to 5 sts before marker, k2tog, k3; rep from * once—184 sts.

Cont in St st and rep Dec rnd [every other rnd] 42 times—16 sts.

Close bottom by grafting tog 8 sts between markers using Kitchener st.

Weave in all ends.

Finished Measurements

16" x 18" after fulling
(excluding strap)

Materials

- Cascade *220* (100% wool; 220 yds/100g per skein): 5 skeins Brown/Black Heather #9412
- Size 10 ½ (6.5mm) double-pointed needles (set of 5) and 24" circular needles
- Stitch markers, 1 in CC for beg of rnd
- Tapestry needle
- 1 antler tip button

Pre-fulling Gauge

15 sts and 20 rnds = 4" (10cm) in St st with single strand of yarn. *Gauge is not critical for this project; make sure that your sts are loose and airy.*

ROSETTES

I ORDERED MY FIRST SET OF ROSETTE IRONS FROM AN ADVERTISEMENT IN THE BACK OF *McCALL'S NEEDLEWORK AND CRAFTS* MAGAZINE. I AM SURE THAT MY MOTHER WAS NERVOUS ABOUT THE HOT OIL COOKING, BUT SHE LET ME MAKE THEM, AND NOW ROSETTE MAKING IS PART OF OUR FAMILY HOLIDAY BAKING ROUTINE.

   2 EGGS

   2 TBSP. GRANULATED SUGAR

   ¼ TSP. SALT

   1 c. MILK

   1 c. ALL-PURPOSE FLOUR

CONFECTIONERS' SUGAR, FOR DUSTING

BEAT EGGS, SUGAR, AND SALT TOGETHER, THEN ADD MILK AND FLOUR AND BEAT UNTIL SMOOTH.

HEAT OIL AND IRON TO 375º F IN DEEP SAUCEPAN. DRAIN IRON AND DIP INTO BATTER TO WITHIN 1/2 INCH OF TOP OF IRON. FRY IN OIL UNTIL CRISP AND LIGHTLY BROWN. IF BATTER SLIPS OFF, IRON IS TOO COLD. REMOVE ROSETTE AND LET DRAIN ON PAPER. ROSETTES CAN BE DUSTED WITH CONFECTIONERS' SUGAR.

FLAP

Pick up and knit 62 sts along the back cast-on edge.

Rows 1, 3, 5 (WS): K5, purl to last 5 sts, k5.

Rows 2, 4, 6 (RS): Knit.

Row 7 (inc): K5, M1, purl to last 5 sts, M1, k5—64 sts.

Row 8: K5, knit to last 5 sts, k5.

Rep [Rows 7 and 8] 6 times—78 sts.

Dec row (RS): K5, ssk, knit to last 7 sts, k2tog, k5—76 sts.

Maintaining est pat with 5 sts of garter at each edge and St st in center, rep Dec row [every other row] 28 times, ending with a WS row—20 sts.

Buttonhole row 1 (RS): K5, ssk, k1, k2tog, yo twice, ssk, k1, k2tog, k5—18 sts.

Buttonhole row 2: K5, p3, k1 in front and back of double yo, p3, k5.

Work Dec row on next, then [every other row] twice more, ending with a WS row—12 sts.

Next row: K4, ssk, k2tog, k4—10 sts.

BO.

STRAP

CO 12 sts.

Row 1: K9, yf, sl 3.

Rep Row 1 until piece measures 6 feet.

BO.

Do not attach strap until after fulling process.

Finishing

Weave in all ends.

Full bag and strap separately in washing machine until they achieve finished measurements or desired size. Rinse and lay flat to dry, pulling fabric as necessary to shape as desired. When pieces are completely dry, sew strap to bag.

Rosemaled Shag Bag

This sturdy bag is knit with a double strand of yarn prior to fulling. Needle felting is used to apply the design since the thickness of the finished bag is much too stiff for hand embroidery.

The idea of adding shag around the top rim of the bag came from a pair of gloves that were from the collection of weaver and world traveler Ruth Ketterer Harris and her husband, Wilfred. Based on the embroidery motifs and colors, the gloves were most likely made in the early twentieth century in Numedal, Buskerud County, Norway.

The familiar *rosemaled* motif was inspired by the embroidery on a pair of mittens that featured four similar motifs. Betsey Toifson Hansen (1867–1958) brought the mittens from Hallingdal, Norway, to Linn Grove, Iowa, in about 1875.

Finished Measurements (after fulling)
Circumference: 28"
Length: 13"

Materials

- Cascade *220* (100% wool; 220yds/100g per skein): 5 skeins Teal #8892 (MC)
- 4 colors of contrasting yarns for needle-felted motif; approx 3 yards of each
- Size 10 ½ (6.5mm) 16" circular needles
- Size 15 (10mm) double-pointed and 24" circular needles
- Tapestry needle
- Stitch markers, 1 in CC for beg of rnd
- Needle-felting needle

Pre-fulled Gauge
13 sts and 18 rnds = 4" (10cm) in St st with larger needles and 2 strands of yarn held tog.
Gauge is not critical for this project; make sure your sts are loose and airy.

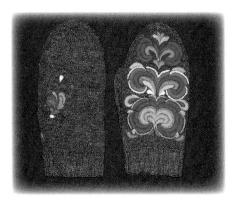

*Mittens brought by
Betsey Toifson Hansen (1867–1958)
from Hallingdal, Norway,
to Linn Grove, Iowa, in about 1875.*

Special Techniques

5-St I-Cord: *K5, do not turn, slip sts back to LH needle; rep from * until cord is desired length. BO.

Fulling: Fulling is the process of shrinking an already-formed fabric by applying moisture, heat, and agitation. For knitted objects, this process is best done in a washing machine set on the hot, heavy-duty, ultra-clean cycle. Add ¼ cup fabric softener and 1 tablespoon vinegar to help the fiber scales open, then close, locking them together. Putting a pair of jeans or a tennis ball into the machine will help increase the agitation. For best results, run the item through the wash cycle only, checking the progress periodically. Allowing the object to go through the spin cycle may put creases in the fabric than can be hard to remove later. Some yarns and colors will need to go through the wash cycle twice or more. When the object has reached the desired size, remove from the machine, rinse in lukewarm water, shape as necessary, and allow to dry thoroughly.

Pattern Notes

- Use double strand of MC throughout construction of the bag.
- Bag is worked in the round; change to double-pointed needles when stitches no longer fit comfortably on circular needle.
- The template for the *rosemaled* motif is shown in the colors used on the sample. Use whatever colors you desire with whatever yarn you have handy—yarn weight is not an issue.
- Needle felting and shag decoration is done after the bag has been fulled to the desired size.

Instructions

With smaller needles and a double strand of yarn, CO 72 sts; pm for beg of rnd and join, taking care not to twist sts.
Knit 14 rnds.

Next rnd (dec): *K1, k2tog; rep from * around—48 sts.

Next rnd (inc): Change to larger needles; knit in the front and back of each st around—96 sts.

Knit every rnd until piece measures 16" from beg.

Setup rnd: *K8, pm; rep from * around.

Dec rnd: *Knit to 2 sts before marker, k2tog; rep from * around—84 sts.

Knit 6 rnds, then rep Dec rnd—72 sts.
Knit 5 rnds, then rep Dec rnd—60 sts.
Knit 4 rnds, then rep Dec rnd—48 sts.
Knit 3 rnds, then rep Dec rnd—36 sts.
Knit 2 rnds, then rep Dec rnd—24 sts.
Knit 1 rnd.

Last rnd: K2tog around—12 sts.

Break yarn, leaving a 12" tail; using tapestry needle, thread tail through rem sts and pull tight.
Weave in all ends.

STRAPS
(make 2)
With a double strand of yarn and larger dpn, CO 5 sts and work
I-cord for 48".
Sew to top of bag in "U" shape before fulling.

Finishing
Full the bag in washing machine until it reaches finished
measurements or desired size.
Apply shag to rim of bag (see photo and sidebar).
Following template, needle-felt *rosemaling* motif on bag
(see illustration and sidebar).

Close up of needle felted bag.

Needle Felting

Stuff the bag with something soft, such as an old sweater;
this will prevent you from poking yourself with the needle-
felting needle.

Apply four colors of yarn (using the same colors you chose for
the shag) to the surface of the felted fabric in the pattern shown
in the Rosemaling Template. "Swirling" the yarns into the shapes
looks good.

Using the barbed needle-felting needle, repeatedly poke the
yarn and fabric until the fibers of the applied yarn have bonded
with the fabric of the bag. It may take numerous poking repetitions
to get the fiber to bond tightly to the bag.

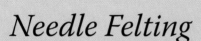

Template for Needle-felted rosemaling on Shag Bag

41

Shag Directions

The shag is applied to the rim of the bag after the fulling process is completed. Four colors (A, B, C, D) are used to create a pattern; the colors used are "knitter's choice."

Lay a pencil or a size 10 dpn along the rim as shown in Step 1 photo. Using a sharp tapestry needle and a double strand of yarn, stitch through the bag and around the needle to make a loop.

Repeat this about 16 times or until the width of the rim is covered (Step 2 photo).

Create loop pattern as follows:

Columns 1 and 2: 16A

Column 3: 16B

Column 4: 6C, 4D, 6C
Repeat Columns 1–4 around the rim of the bag.

Using sharp-tipped scissors, slide blade into center of loops and clip them as shown in Step 3 photo.

Step 1

Step 2

Step 3

Beaded Fjord Shawl

Finished Measurements
Approx. 72" wide x 39"
long (blocked)

Materials

- Misti International *Hand Paint Worsted* (100% baby alpaca; 218 yds/100g per skein): 3 skeins Neruda #WP06
- Size 9 (5.5mm) 36" circular needle or size needed to obtain gauge
- Approx 250 size 6 beads (clear)
- Bead threader
- Tapestry needle

Gauge
14 sts and 24 rows = 4" (10cm) in garter stitch (blocked).
Note: For larger shawl, use larger needles/gauge; for smaller shawl, use smaller needles/gauge.

The color palette of this shawl and its beaded edges remind us of the water in one very captivating fjord painting displayed in Vesterheim. The blues and greens in this painting are represented in all their ice-formed grandeur in the Hand Paint yarn from Misti International. I hope that you get lost in these colors and in the beauty of the alpaca yarn, just as we did.

Pattern Notes
- If you discover that you haven't threaded enough beads and need to add more, you can always either break your yarn and spit-splice (see sidebar) the other end of the skein and thread more beads.
- Take advantage of the spit-splice technique to join skeins.

Instructions
Using bead threader, thread approx ¼ of the beads onto each skein.
Leaving a 6" tail, CO 1 st.
Row 1: Slide bead up, yo, knit to end of row.
Rep Row 1 until you've almost run out of yarn or shawl is desired size.
BO very loosely.
Using tail from cast-on, add 1 more bead to point of shawl, then weave in tail.
Weave in rem tails.
Block to desired size, pinning out beaded yo's.

FJORD SHAWL TIP

TIFFANY TEST-KNITTED THE

SHAWL AND HAD A GREAT TIP:

STRING ALL THE BEADS ON

ONE SKEIN AND

SPIT-SPLICE THE SKEINS

TOGETHER, BEING CAREFUL

TO SPLICE NEATLY SO THAT

THE BEADS WILL SLIDE.

Spit-Splicing of Yarn

by Kate Martinson

One of the basic techniques our forebears employed that is no longer in general practice is the splicing of yarn when creating looped fabrics. Whether one is *nålbinding*, knitting, or crocheting, connecting one end of yarn to the next with a knot will not provide the strongest join because the knot impedes the movement necessary for most looped fabric. Some people avoid a knot by leaving a few inches of the new and old ends loose, returning later to sew the tails into the back of the fabric; however, this method often creates a bump, a weak spot, and a change in the face of at least one side of the fabric. Easier by far is simply to splice the two ends together.

To splice two yarns together, fray the ends of each yarn for at least 2 inches. Do not merely separate the plies or individual threads of a multistrand yarn—the individual fibers must be completely separated, creating a very fuzzy end. Next, overlap the unspun fibers of the two ends and lay them across the palm of your less dominant hand (left for right-handers, right for left-handers). Lick the palm of the other hand, depositing a generous amount of saliva. Place your two palms together, apply pressure, and vigorously roll the yarn back and forth. The combination of the saliva, the frayed ends, and the friction should successfully "felt" the two ends together. This splice should last as long as your garment does.

The colors in "Depth of the Fjord", an oil painting by Floyd Johnson, Minneapolis, Minnesota, 1980, provided the inspiration for the Fjord Shawl. VESTERHEIM MUSEUM COLLECTION

3

Two-Color Knitting

T his chapter, which showcases projects that use two-color knitting as the primary means of decoration, is, not surprisingly, the largest chapter in the book. Most of the projects are worked in the round or worked by knitting every row, making it much easier to follow a charted pattern. The motifs used, which were drawn from historical pieces, illustrate a variety of common symbols. Some of the projects, like the knapsack, offer an updated use of the traditional pattern.

Cross-Country Ski Hat

Size
Adult average

Finished Measurements
Inside Circumference: 20"
Length (brim to crown): 9 ½"

Materials

- Dale of Norway *Heilo* (100% wool; 109 yds/50g per skein): *Green/Gold colorway:* 2 skeins Olive #8972 (MC) and 1 skein Goldenrod #2427 (CC)
- Size 4 (3.5mm) 16" circular needle
- Size 5 (3.75mm) double-pointed needles (set of 5) and 16" circular needles or size needed to obtain gauge
- Size F/5 (3.75mm) crochet hook
- Stitch marker
- Tapestry needle

Gauge
24 sts and 26 rnds = 4" (10cm) in stranded 2-color St st with larger needles.
Adjust needle size as necessary to obtain correct gauge.

One of our favorite items in the collection is a pair of blue and white Nordic ski socks. The socks are well worn, or well loved, depending upon your point of view. The frayed areas and holes do not take away from the fact that they are beautifully crafted.

The patterning on the calf gusset was the first thing to grab our designer's eye. Its diminishing diamond pattern was perfect for the crown of a hat. The alternating snowflake patterns on the sock included one very common eight-point star and another not-so-common four-diamond motif that is used in the main band of the hat.

Special Technique

Provisional Cast-On: With crochet hook and waste yarn, make a chain several sts longer than desired cast-on. With knitting needle and project yarn, pick up indicated number of sts in the "bumps" on back of chain. When indicated in pattern, "unzip" the crochet chain to free live sts.

Pattern Notes

- The hat is worked in the round; change to double-pointed needles when stitches no longer fit comfortably on circular needle.
- The facing is worked on a smaller needle to get a tighter fit; after brim pattern is complete, the facing is folded inside hat and fused to brim using a 3-needle join technique.

Sock, no history available.
LUTHER COLLEGE COLLECTION

*Othelia Melbraaten Rosendahl and
Anna Sylling on skis, Houston County,
Minnesota, early 1900s.*
ROSENDAHL COLLECTION,
VESTERHEIM ARCHIVE

Instructions

FACING

With smaller needle and MC, using provisional method, CO 130 sts; pm for beg of rnd and join, taking care not to twist sts.
Knit 26 rnds.
Next 2 rnds (turning ridge): Purl.

BRIM

Change to larger needle.
Knit 1 rnd.
Work 21 rnds following Chart A.
Next rnd (3-needle join): Place CO sts on smaller needle and fold facing inside brim so that WS are together. (The larger needle with brim sts should be on the outside and the smaller needle with facing sts should be lined up on the inside of the hat). Holding needles parallel and using MC, *knit tog 1 st from the front needle and 1 from the back needle; rep from * around until all sts are joined.
Next 3 rnds: With MC, purl and inc 2 sts evenly spaced on the last rnd—132 sts.

CROWN

With MC, knit 1 rnd.
Work 18 rnds following Chart B.
Rnd 19 (dec): Maintaining the charted pat throughout decreasing, *k1, ssk, k7, k2tog; rep from * around—110 sts.
Rnds 20–26: Work even.
Rnd 27 (dec): *K1, ssk, k5, k2tog; rep from * around—88 sts.
Rnds 28–33: Work even.
Rnd 34 (dec): *K1, ssk, k3, k2tog; rep from * around—66 sts.
Rnds 35–38: Work even.
Rnd 39 (dec): *K1, ssk, k1, k2tog; rep from * around—44 sts.
Rnd 40: Work even. Break CC.
Rnd 41 (dec): *K1, S2KP2; rep from * around—22 sts.
Rnd 42: Knit.
Break yarn, leaving a 6" tail.
With tapestry needle, thread tail through rem sts, pull tight, and leave tail for securing braided tassel.

BRAIDED TASSEL

Cut 12 [16"] pieces of MC and 8 [16"] pieces of CC.
Create two bundles of yarn with 6 MC and 4 CC in each bundle. Tie one end of the bundle and make fishtail braid (see p. 87) until 2" of yarn rem. Tie overhand knot. Rep for 2nd braid. Fold both braids in half using tail at top of hat, secure to hat.

Finishing Weave in all ends. Block.

CHART B: CROWN

12-st rep, dec to 2-st rep

CHART A: BRIM

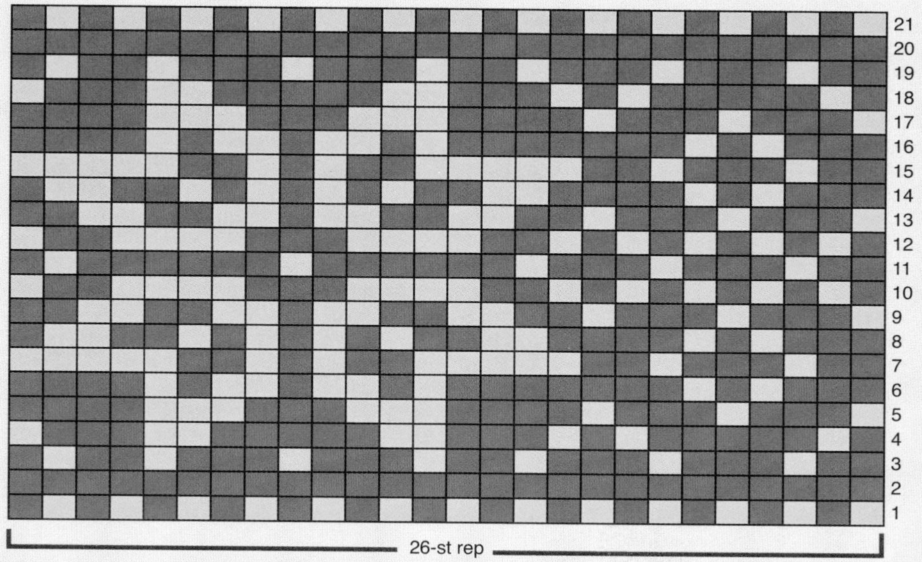

26-st rep

STITCH AND COLOR KEY

- Knit MC
- Knit CC
- K2tog MC
- Ssk MC
- S2KP2 MC

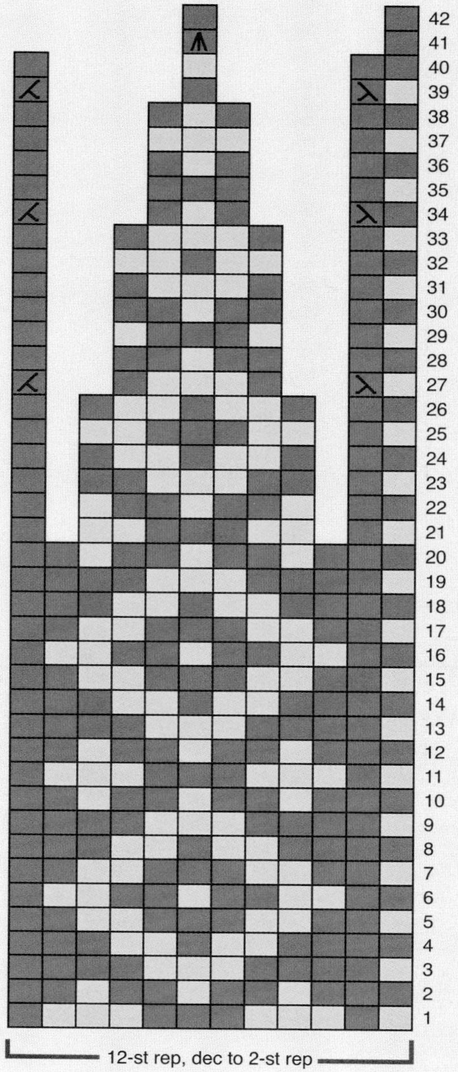

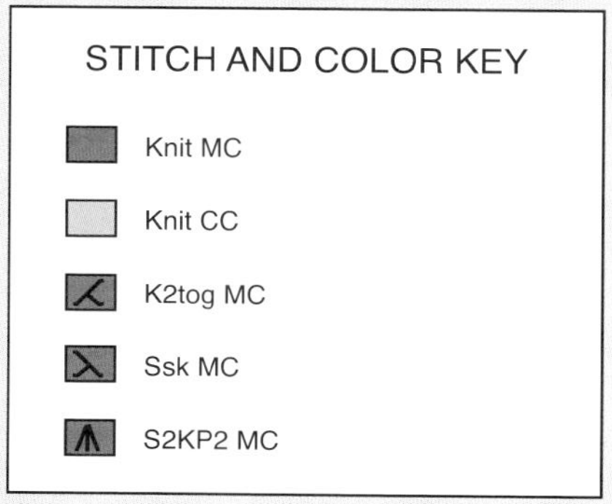

Cross-Country Ski Socks

Size
1 Size: Woman's large/
Man's medium

Finished Measurements
Length from cuff to ankle: 16"
Foot circumference: 9"

Materials

- Raumagarn *Gammelserie*
  (100% wool; 174 yds /50g per
  ball): 3 balls Steel Blue #438
  (MC), 2 balls Natural White
  #401 (CC)
- Size 1 (2.25mm) double-
  pointed needles (set of 5)
- Size 2 (2.75mm) double-
  pointed needles (set of 5) or
  size needed to obtain gauge
- Stitch markers, 1 in CC for beg
  of rnd
- Tapestry needle

Gauge
34 sts and 40 rnds = 4" (10cm) in
stranded 2-color St st on
larger dpns.
*Adjust needle size as necessary to
obtain correct gauge.*

Judging from the generous calf diameter of the original socks, one can imagine strong legs taking numerous trips up and down the mountains of Norway. A few changes were made to the original sock pattern. First, to make it more knittable and easier to chart, the snowflake repeats were balanced so that they match up along the entire length of the sock. Second, the dividing lines were changed to solid instead of the alternating pattern of the original piece. This reduced the number of long contrasting yarn carries inside the sock. Third, we added more decreases to the center pattern in the calf since the original sock's ankle was much too baggy. Removing the solid white section at the cuff was the final modification.

The sock is knit with a Norwegian yarn from Rauma called *Gammelserie*, or old series, which is crisp and not too fuzzy. It also allowed a gauge that would accommodate all the patterns in the sock.

Special Abbreviations

N1, N2, N3, N4: Needle 1, needle 2, needle 3, needle 4, with N1 and N4 holding gusset/sole sts and N2 and N3 holding instep sts.

Pattern Stitch

Salt and Pepper pat (S&P)
Knit back and forth for heel flap:
Row 1 (RS): *K1 CC, k1 MC, rep from * across.
Row 2: *P1 CC, p1 MC, rep from * across.
Knit circularly for sole:
Rnd 1: *K1 CC, k1 MC, rep from * around.
Rnd 2: *K1 MC, k1 CC, rep from * around.
Rep Rows/Rnds 1 and 2 for pat.

Pattern Notes

- Shaped Sock Calf gusset section is charted with the increases and decreases.
- Each charted pattern is separated by a column of CC stitches that creates vertical lines; these stitches do not appear in the charts but will be referred to in the pattern text as "k1 CC."
- All M1 increases are made with MC.
- When working foot, the Salt and Pepper heel pattern is continued through the sole, and patterns from leg are continued on the instep. The left and right edges of instep are partial Chart C panels; beginning and ending points for these sections are indicated on the chart.
- Carry stranded yarn loosely to maintain elasticity of sock.
- Weave in yarn not in use when carrying it more than 5 sts to avoid long floats inside socks.

Close up of calf gusset, ski sock.

Instructions

CUFF
With smaller dpns and MC, CO 104 sts, pm for beg of rnd and join, taking care not to twist sts.
Work k1, p1 Rib for 2".

LEG
Change to larger dpns.
Rnd 1 (setup): K1 CC, work Chart A over 3 sts, k1 CC, work Chart B over 15 sts, k1 CC, work Chart C over 19 sts, k1 CC, Chart B (15 sts), k1 CC, Chart C (19 sts), k1 CC, Chart B (15 sts), k1 CC, Chart A (3 sts), k1 CC, Chart D (7 sts).
Rnds 2–23 (Calf Gusset incs): Cont to work charts in est pat with 1-st CC columns separating sections; rep Charts B, C, and D as needed along the length of the sock; M1 incs are made in Chart A sections on Rnds 3, 8, 15, and 23 as indicated on chart—120 sts.
Rnds 24–48: Work even following charts.
Rnds 49–78 (Calf Gusset decs): Work charts in est pats,

decreasing in Chart A sections on Rnds 49, 57, 65, 75, and 78 as indicated on chart—100 sts.

Rnds 79–80: K1 CC, k1 MC, k1 CC, Chart B (15 sts), k1 CC, Chart C (19 sts), k1 CC, Chart B (15 sts), k1 CC, Chart C (19 sts), k1 CC, Chart B (15 sts), k1 CC, k1 MC, k1 CC, Chart D (7 sts), k1 CC.

Rnd 81: K3tog CC, Chart B, k1 CC, Chart C, k1 CC, Chart B, k1 CC, Chart C, k1 CC, Chart B, ssk CC, Chart D, end with Rnd 3 of Chart D—96 sts.

Note: Chart E will now be substituted for Chart D for the rem dec rnds.

Rnds 82–99 (Back-Leg Panel decs): K1 CC, Chart B, k1 CC, Chart C, k1 CC, Chart B, k1 CC, Chart C, k1 CC, Chart B, k1 CC, Chart E, decreasing in Chart E section on Rnds 86, 93 and 99 as indicated on chart—90 sts.

Rnds 100–132: K1 CC, Chart B, k1 CC, Chart C, k1 CC, Chart B, k1 CC, Chart C, k1 CC, Chart B; work even until 5th snowflake is complete on Chart B on Rnd 2.

HEEL FLAP

Setup rnd: Work Salt and Pepper pat over first 23 sts, place next 45 sts on hold on 2 dpns for instep, turn—45 sts rem for heel.

Row 1 (WS): P1 MC, work S&P pat as est to last st, p1 MC.
Work even for 3" in est S&P pat, maintaining first and last st in MC on all rows, ending with a WS row.

TURN HEEL

Note: Maintain S&P pat throughout.

Row 1: Work 26 sts in est pat, ssk, k1, turn.

Row 2: Sl 1, p8, p2tog, p1, turn.

Row 3: Sl 1, k9, ssk, k1, turn.

Row 4: Sl 1, p10, p2tog, p1, turn

Cont working in this manner, working 1 more st on each row until all sts have been worked, ending with a WS row—27 sts.

GUSSET

Setup rnd: With RS facing, work 14 sts in est pat; with N1, work rem 13 sts of heel flap, then with MC and CC, continuing S&P pat, pick up and knit 16 sts along the left edge of heel; with N2 and N3, work across instep sts in est pat from leg; with N4, working S&P pat so that it will flow into heel pat, pick up and knit 16 sts along right edge of heel, work first 14 heel sts in pat; pm for new beg of rnd—104 sts with 29 sts on N1, 45 sts on N2 and N3 combined, 30 sts on N4.

Rnd 1: N1: Work in est S&P pat to last 3 sts, k2tog MC, k1 CC; N2 and N3: work Chart C in est pat (starting at "Beg Right Instep" as indicated on chart), k1 CC, work Chart B, k1 CC, work Chart C in est pat (ending at "End Left Instep" as indicated on chart); N4: k1 CC, ssk MC, work in est S&P pat to end—102 sts.

Rnd 2: Knit in pats as charted.

Rep [Rnds 1 and 2] 6 more times—90 sts.

FOOT

Work even in est pats until foot measures 8" from back of heel or 2 ¼" short of desired length.

TOE

Rnd 1: N1: Knit in pat to last 3 sts, k2tog MC, k1 CC; N2: ssk MC, work S&P pat to end; N3: work S&P pat to last 2 sts, k2tog MC; N4: k1 CC, ssk MC, work to end—86 sts.

Rep [Rnd 1] every rnd 20 times—6 sts.

Break yarns.

With tapestry needle and MC tail, run tail through 1 set of 2 MC sts, forming stripe to complete dec line, then bring tapestry needle and tail through sock to other set of 2 MC sts, run tail through the 2 sts; secure tail to WS. With tapestry needle and CC tail, run tail through 2 CC sts and secure to WS.

Weave in all ends.

Block.

Nordic ski socks.

Men skiing, Houston County, Minnesota, early 1900s.
ROSENDAHL COLLECTION, VESTERHEIM ARCHIVE

STITCH AND COLOR KEY

- ▦ K with MC
- ☐ K with CC
- ◩ SSK with MC
- ◪ K2tog with MC
- ⟁ S2KP2 with MC
- Ⓜ M1 with MC
- ◆ On Chart B, end here after 5th star is complete

CHART E

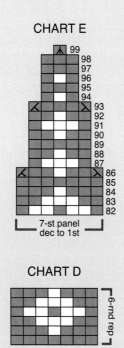

7-st panel
dec to 1st

CHART D

7-st panel

6-rnd rep

CHART C

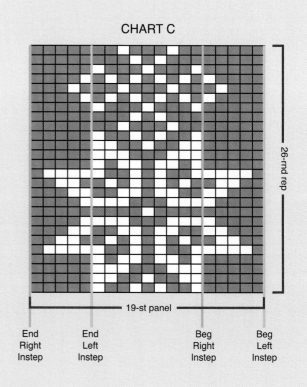

26-rnd rep

19-st panel

End Right Instep | End Left Instep | Beg Right Instep | Beg Left Instep

CHART A

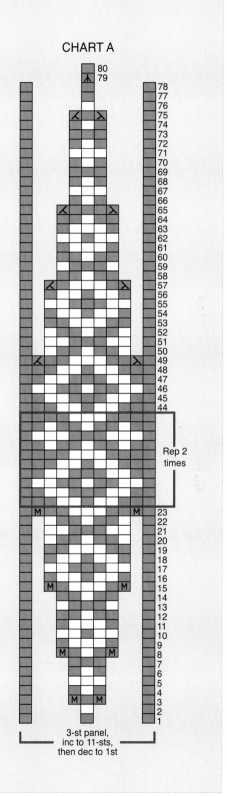

3-st panel,
inc to 11-sts,
then dec to 1st

CHART B

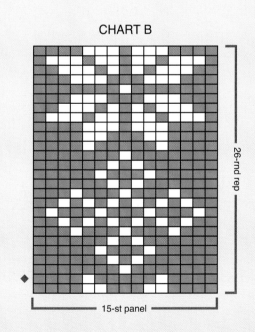

26-rnd rep

15-st panel

Kloster Block Headband

The Kloster block is a familiar pattern in Hardanger embroidery. Normally, there is some thread-cutting involved in the making of Hardanger. The trim on the cuffs and collar of the Voss blouse (see page 57) inspired the pattern in the headband.

Special Technique
Provisional Cast-On: With crochet hook and waste yarn, make a chain several sts longer than desired cast-on. With knitting needle and project yarn, pick up indicated number of sts in the "bumps" on back of chain. When indicated in pattern, "unzip" the crochet chain to free live sts.

Pattern Note
The Kloster Block pattern is created by knitting the first row of the block, then purling the next 2 rows.

Instructions

OUTER BAND
Using provisional method, larger needle, and MC, CO 112 sts; pm for beg of rnd and join, taking care not to twist sts.
Knit 1 rnd, purl 1 rnd.
Work 17 rnds following Kloster Block Chart; break CC.
Knit 1 rnd, purl 1 rnd.

LINING
Change to smaller needle and knit 18 rnds.
Unzip provisional cast-on, placing live sts onto larger needle.
Fold headband with WS tog, then join outer band and lining using Kitchener st.

Finishing
Block to finished measurements.

This Voss blouse was made in the late 1800s by Ingeborg Larsdatter Lillethum of Vossestrand, Voss, Hordaland County, Norway. She immigrated to Boone County, Illinois, in 1909.

Kloster Block Headband Chart

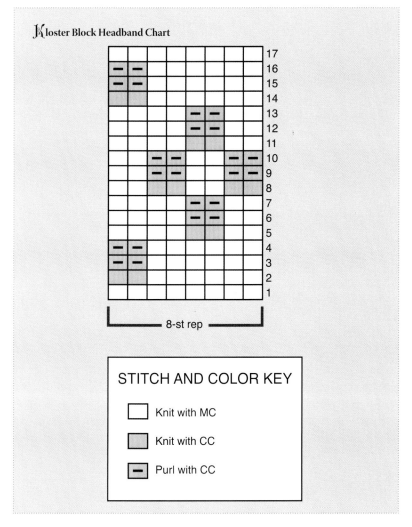

8-st rep

STITCH AND COLOR KEY

☐ Knit with MC

▦ Knit with CC

▦— Purl with CC

Reindeer Headband

Finished Measurements
Circumference: 20"
Width: 2 ½"

Materials

- Blackberry Ridge *Mer-Made DK Wool* (100% superwash merino wool; 260 yds/114g [4 oz] per ball): 1 ball each Black (MC) and Natural Cream (CC)
- Size 6 (4mm) 16" circular needle
- Size 7 (4.5mm) 16" circular needle or size needed to obtain gauge
- Size G/7 (4.5mm) crochet hook

Gauge
22 sts and 28 rnds = 4" (10cm) in stranded 2-color St st with larger needle.
Adjust needle size as necessary to obtain correct gauge.

Herds of domesticated reindeer have long been an important part of survival in northern Norway, providing milk, meat, hides, and antlers to the native Arctic people.

Special Technique
Provisional Cast-On: With crochet hook and waste yarn, make a chain several sts longer than desired cast-on. With knitting needle and project yarn, pick up indicated number of sts in the "bumps" on back of chain. When indicated in pattern, "unzip" the crochet chain to free live sts.

Instructions
OUTER BAND
With MC and larger needle, using provisional method, CO 114 sts; pm for beg of rnd and join, taking care not to twist sts.
Knit 1 rnd, purl 1 rnd.
Work 18 rnds following Reindeer Chart; break CC.
Knit 1 rnd, purl 1 rnd.

LINING

Change to smaller needle and knit 20 rnds.

Unzip provisional cast-on, placing live sts onto larger needle.

Fold headband with WS tog, then join outer band and lining using Kitchener st.

Finishing

Block to finished measurements.

This embroidered pillow cover, which inspired the reindeer headband, was made by Mrs. Valdemar Holm of Seattle, Washington, in 1937. It was donated to Vesterheim in 1974.

Reindeer Headband Chart

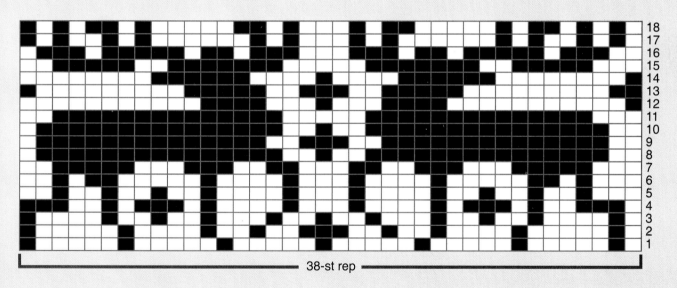

38-st rep

COLOR KEY

■ MC

□ CC

Rose or Bridal Wimple

The wimple has its origins in the Near East and was worn as a fashion accessory by women in medieval Europe following the Crusades. It survives to this day as part of the habits worn by nuns from certain orders. Modern women living in chilly northern climates also wear wimples to keep warm in the winter.

The two charted designs choices are from some of the many Selbu mittens at Vesterheim.

Bridal Whimple

Finished Measurements
Circumference (main section): Approx. 26"
Length: Approx. 21"

Materials

- *Rose version:* Raumagarn *Røros Lamullgarn* (100% wool; 273 yds/50g per skein): 4 skeins Light Gray #12 (2 strands held together = MC); 1 skein each Light Blue #67 and Medium Blue #68 (blues held tog = CC)

- *Bridal version:* Misti International *Misti Alpaca Sport* (100% alpaca; 146 yds/50g per skein): 3 skeins Natural Dark Brown #NT408 (MC) and 1 skein Golden Spice #MR6213
- Size 6 (4mm) 24" circular needle or 1 size smaller than size needed to obtain gauge
- Size 7 (4.5mm) 24" circular needle or size needed to obtain gauge
- Stitch markers, 1 in CC for beg of rnd
- Tapestry needle

Gauge
20 sts and 22 rnds = 4" (10cm) in stranded 2-color St st with larger needle; for Rose version, 2 strands of yarn are held tog throughout. *Adjust needle size as necessary to obtain correct gauge.*

Pattern Stitch
Lace (multiple of 8 sts)
Rnd 1: [K1, yo, k1, k2tog, p1, ssk, k1, yo] 26 times.
Rnd 2: [K4, p1, k3] 26 times.
Rep Rnds 1 and 2 for pat.

These gloves (ca. 1900) provided the inspiration for the rose whimple. They belonged to Lully Hansen Lund, who immigrated from Drammen, Norway, to Fargo, North Dakota, in 1919.

Pattern Notes
- The Rose version is worked with two strands of yarn held together; the two blue yarns held together create the contrasting color (CC).
- If desired, place markers between each lace repeat.
- Take care with tension when working stranded stockinette stitch; if necessary, change to smaller needle size when working plain stockinette stitch to match gauge of pattern section.

Instructions

LACE BORDER

With larger needle and MC, CO 208 sts; pm for beg of rnd and join, taking care not to twist sts.
Purl 1 rnd.
Work 24 rnds in lace pat.

MAIN SECTION

Knit 1 rnd, placing markers every 13 sts.
Dec rnd: *Knit to 2 sts before marker, k2tog; rep from * around—192 sts.
Next rnd: Knit.
Rep [last 2 rnds] 3 times more—144 sts.
Rose version only
Next rnd: *Knit to marker, [knit to 2 sts before next marker, k2tog] 7 times; rep from * once more—130 sts.
Bridal version only
Next rnd: Rep Dec rnd—128 sts.
Knit 1 rnd, rearranging markers as follows: *Rose pat:* every 13 sts; *Bridal pat:* every 16 sts.
Work chart for either Roses or Bridal pat as desired, removing markers on last rnd.
With MC, work even in St st until piece measures 15" from end of lace pat or to desired length.
With smaller needle, work k1, p1 Rib for 1".
Bind off very loosely in rib.

Finishing
Weave in all ends.
Block to finished measurements, opening up lace section as desired.

BRIDAL CHART

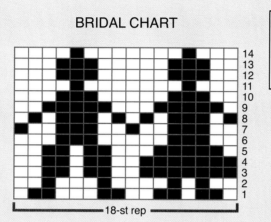

18-st rep

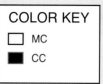

COLOR KEY

☐ MC
■ CC

ROSE CHART

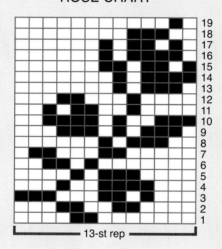

13-st rep

LACE CHART

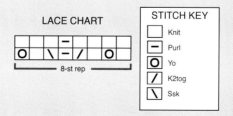

8-st rep

STITCH KEY

☐	Knit
−	Purl
O	Yo
/	K2tog
\	Ssk

63

Rose or Bridal Wristers

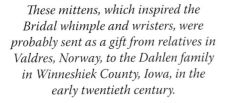

These mittens, which inspired the Bridal whimple and wristers, were probably sent as a gift from relatives in Valdres, Norway, to the Dahlen family in Winneshiek County, Iowa, in the early twentieth century.

Using elements of the Selbu mittens, these wristers are a fast, fun version of the very modern fingerless mitten. Also called pulse warmers, these wristers are just that. Wear them so that the ribbing hugs your hand and keeps the wind from rushing up your sleeves, or wear them with the lace peeking out from your cuff. Wear them together with the matching wimple and have a warm soul and warm hands.

Size
Woman's average

Finished Measurement
Circumference: 8"

Materials

- Dale of Norway *Baby Ull* (100% superwash merino wool; 180 yds/50g per skein): *(Rose version)* 1 skein each Turquoise #6714 (MC) and White #0010 (CC) or *(Bridal)* 1 skein each Navy #5755 (MC) and Green #9436 (CC)
- Size 2 (2.75mm) double-pointed needles or size needed to obtain gauge
- Stitch markers, 1 in CC for beg of rnd
- Tapestry needle

Gauge
32 sts and 36 rnds = 4" (10cm) in stranded 2-color St st.
Adjust needle size as necessary to obtain correct gauge.

Pattern Stitch

Lace (multiple of 8 sts)
Rnd 1: [K1, yo, k1, k2tog, p1, ssk, k1, yo] 7 times.
Rnd 2: [K4, p1, k3] 7 times.
Rep Rnds 1 and 2 for pat.

Pattern Note

These wristers are designed so that Rose/Bridal pattern will be correctly oriented when lace is worn at wrist; if you prefer ribbing at wrist, work Rose/Bridal chart upside down so that it will be oriented correctly when worn.

Instructions

STRIPED LACE EDGE (both versions)
With MC, CO 56 sts; pm for beg of rnd and join, taking care not to twist sts.
Purl 1 rnd, placing markers every 8 sts.
Work Lace pat in following stripe sequence: 4 rnds MC, 1 rnd CC, 1 rnd MC, 2 rnds CC, 1 rnd MC, 1 rnd CC, 1 rnd MC, 2 rnds CC, 1 rnd MC, 1 rnd CC, 4 rnds MC, ending with Rnd 1 of pat.
Removing markers, with MC, knit around and inc 1 st—57 sts.
Knit 2 rnds.
Work 4 rnds following Rings Chart.
Continue as follows for desired pattern (Rose or Bridal).

Rose Wrister
Inc rnd: With MC, k4, [M1, k7] 7 times, M1, k4—65 sts.
Work 18 rnds following Rose Chart on pg 63.
With MC, knit 1 rnd.
Dec rnd: K4, [k2tog, k6] 7 times, k2tog, k3—57 sts.

Bridal Wrister
Inc rnd: With MC, k3, [M1, k7] 7 times, M1, k4—64 sts.
Work 13 rnds following Bridal Chart on pg 63.
With MC, knit 1 rnd.
Dec rnd: K3, [k2tog, k6] 7 times, k2tog, k3—57 sts.

RIBBED EDGE (both versions)
Work 4 rnds following Rings Chart.
With MC, knit around and dec 1 st—56 st.
Next 4 rnds: *K2 MC, p2 CC; rep from * around.
With MC, bind off knitwise.

Finishing

Weave in all ends.
Block.

Rose Wrister

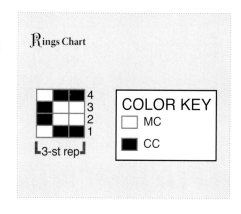

Rings Chart

4
3
2
1

3-st rep

COLOR KEY
☐ MC
■ CC

Daddy Long Legs Mittens

Size
Woman's large

Finished Measurements
Hand Circumference: 9 ½"
Length: 11 ½"

Materials

- Raumagarn *Gammelserie* (100% wool; 174 yds/50g per ball): 2 balls White #GL400 (MC) and 1 ball Brown/Black #GL410 (CC)
- Size 1 (2.25mm) double-pointed needles (set of 5) or size needed to obtain gauge
- Very fine cotton waste yarn
- Stitch markers, 1 in CC for beg of rnd
- Tapestry needle

Gauge
36 sts and 40 rnds = 4" (10cm) in stranded 2-color St st.
Adjust needle size as necessary to obtain correct gauge.

Back of mitten

Our version of a Selbu mitten is a combination of several mittens at Vesterheim. In trying to decide which one to knit, we added together all of our favorite elements—interchangeable motifs for cuffs, lace edge, and unique thumb shaping—to create one fantastic mitten. You will want to knit this great style in other colors and with other motif options.

Pattern Notes
- The color pattern is worked using the "stranded" method, i.e., by carrying both colors at once. Avoid long floats on the inside of the mitten in those areas where more than 5 consecutive stitches are worked in one color by catching the color not in use with the working color.
- The main chart shows the left-hand mitten; to make a right-hand mitten, work Rnds 1–29 of the Right Palm Chart (below the main chart), then continue with the main chart.

Instructions

LEFT MITTEN

Cuff
With MC, CO 64 sts, distribute evenly on 4 dpns, pm for beg of rnd and join, taking care not to twist sts.
Rnd 1: Purl.
Rnd 2: [K1, yo, k1, k2tog, p1, ssk, k1, yo] 8 times around.
Rnd 3: [K4, p1, k3] 8 times around.
Rep Rnds 2 and 3 once more.
Knit 1 rnd.
Next 19 rnds: Join CC and work 16-st Cuff Chart 4 times around. With MC, knit 2 rnds.

Inc rnd: Knit and inc 22 sts evenly around—86 sts.

Next rnd: P78, pm, p7, pm, p1.

Thumb Gusset

Join CC and work Mitten Chart.

Rnds 4, 7, 10, 13, 16, 19, 22, 25 (inc): Work thumb gusset inc as follows: Work in charted pat to first marker, slip marker, M1 with CC, work in pat to next marker, M1 with CC, slip marker, k1—2 sts inc'd each rnd, with 23 thumb gusset sts between markers after last inc.

Rnd 30: Knit in pat to marker; with cotton waste yarn, k23 thumb sts; slip those sts back to LH needle; cont working charted pat over thumb sts and to end of rnd—102 sts.

Main Mitten

Work even following chart through Rnd 66, and on last rnd, k5, pm, k45, pm, k5, pm, k47.

Rnd 66: Work following chart to 3rd marker, ssk MC, knit to last 2 sts, k2tog MC—100 sts.

Top Dec rnd: Following chart, *k5, ssk MC, knit to 2 sts before next marker, k2tog MC; rep from * once—96 sts.

Rep Top Dec rnd [every rnd] 20 times—16 sts.

Break yarn, leaving a 6" tail.

With tapestry needle, thread tail through rem sts twice, pull tight, and secure to WS.

Thumb

Remove cotton waste yarn and place live upper and lower sts on needles—46 sts.

Rnd 1: Beg with original gusset sts, M1 with CC for side st, work 23 sts following Thumb Chart, pm, M1 with MC for side st, work 23 sts in pat to end; pm for beg of rnd—48 sts.

Dec rnd: Following chart, *knit side st, ssk CC, work to 2 sts before marker, k2tog CC; rep from * once more—44 sts.

Rep Dec rnd [every rnd] 3 times—32 sts.

Work even in charted pat through Rnd 18.

Dec rnd: Following chart, *work 2 sts, ssk MC, work to 3 sts before marker, k2tog MC, k1 CC, slip marker; rep from * once—28 sts.

Rep Dec rnd [every other rnd] 5 times more—8 sts.

Work 1 rnd even, then break yarn, leaving a 6" tail.

With tapestry needle, thread tail through rem sts twice, pull tight, and secure to WS.

Weave in all ends.

Block to finished measurements.

RIGHT MITTEN

Work cuff as for Left Mitten.

Thumb Gusset

On purl rnd, place markers as follows: p56, pm, p7, pm, p23. Work as for Right Mitten but follow Left Palm Chart for thumb gusset. When finished with thumb gusset, complete as for Right Mitten.

These mittens were probably sent from relatives in Selbu, Norway, to Edna Eidem in Minneapolis.

The Story of the Selbu Star

Historians generally agree that the Selbu star, or snowflake mitten, was the first two-color work to appear in Norway. As the story goes, Marit, a young farm girl from Selbu, Norway, created the first pair of two-color mittens featuring the Selbu star pattern. She wore these warm mittens to church and caused great enthusiasm among the parishioners.

One can imagine how exciting it was for the local knitters to get their first glimpse of a pair of Selbu mittens. As knitters in Norway took up the challenge of two-color knitting, they drew their designs from a much deeper textile heritage of weaving and embroidery.

MAIN MITTEN CHART

Left Palms: 31 sts inc to 47 sts — Side 5 sts — Back: 45 sts — Side 5 sts

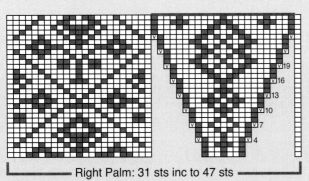

Right Palm: 31 sts inc to 47 sts

CUFF CHART

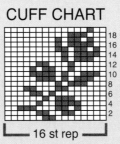

16 st rep

THUMB CHART

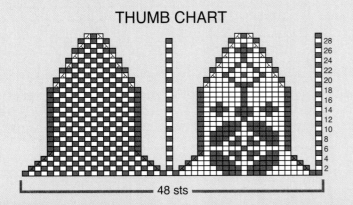

48 sts

STITCH AND COLOR KEY

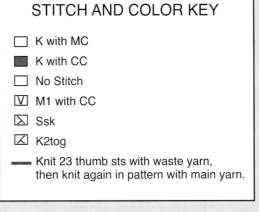

☐ K with MC

■ K with CC

☐ No Stitch

Ⅴ M1 with CC

⧄ Ssk

⧅ K2tog

— Knit 23 thumb sts with waste yarn,
then knit again in pattern with main yarn.

ℕorwegian Knapsack

Materials

- Dale of Norway *Heilo* (100% wool; 109yds/50g per ball): 3 balls Black #0090 (MC) and 2 balls either Red #4018 (CC) or Off-White #0017 (CC)
- Size 5 (3.75mm) double-pointed and 24" circular needles or size needed to obtain gauge
- Tapestry needle
- Stitch markers, 1 in CC for beg of rnd
- Yarn in 3 additional colors to match braid (or as desired if using leather straps) for draw-string and embroidery
- One toggle
- *Option 1:* One set of 36" back-pack straps from Homestead Heirlooms
- *Option 2:* Two yards 1"-wide Norwegian braid for straps
- *Option 2:* 36" separating zipper
- *Option 2:* ½ yard of wool fabric for lining and straps
- *Option 2:* Sewing machine

Gauge

24 sts and 30 rnds = 4" (10cm) in 2-color stranded St st.
Adjust needle size as necessary to obtain correct gauge.

Imagine trekking through the mountains of Norway with this beautiful knapsack on your back. The inspiration for the star (or snow-flake) pattern is from a pair of gloves that were donated to Vesterheim in 1950. Selbu is believed to be the birthplace of two-color knitting in Norway, and the Selbu star has become a widely recognized motif in Norwegian knitting.

The directions offer two options. Option 1 is the "less finishing" version, which uses purchased leather straps and has no lining. Option 2 is the "more finishing" version, which uses the traditional Nor-wegian braid sewn onto wool straps with a separating zipper and wool lining. The instructions are written for Option 1 with notes added for Option 2.

Special Techniques

Kumihimo Braid: See sidebar on page 73.

Pattern Notes

- The bottom of the bag is knit back and forth, then stitches are picked up around the bag, and the rest of the bag is knit circularly.
- The stitch pattern used for the bottom of the bag may seem familiar—it is the slip stitch pattern often used for sock heels and is a very strong, sturdy stitch.
- *Option 1:* Leather straps are sewn onto the outside, so no strap-insertion holes are necessary.

These Selbu star gloves, made in Norway, ca. 1950, were the inspiration for the Norwegian Knapsack.

The knapsack in red

- *Option 2* Large buttonhole-like slots are made for strap-insertion points.
- The drawstring uses a braiding technique called Kumihimo; instructions are shown in separate technique box on page 73.

Instructions

DRAWSTRING

With desired colors of yarn, make Kumihimo drawstring approx. 40" long or to desired length (see sidebar). Set aside.

BOTTOM

With circular needle and MC, cast on 70 sts.

Row 1: Sl 1, purl to end.

Row 2: *Sl 1, k1; rep from * to end.

Rep [Rows 1 and 2] 19 times.

BODY OF BAG

Pickup rnd: *(Both options):* Pick up and knit 20 sts along short side of bottom; *Option 1:* pick up and knit 70 sts along cast-on edge; or *Option 2, create a slot for attaching straps later:* pick up and knit 28 sts along cast-on edge, cast on 14 sts, skip the next 14 sts along the cast-on edge, then pick up and knit 28 sts to corner of bottom; *Both options:* pick up and knit 20 sts along second side of bottom; pm for beg of rnd and join—180 sts.

Rnd 1: Knit.

Rnd 2: Purl.

Set up new beg of rnd: Remove beg of rnd marker, k18, pm for new beg of rnd.

Join CC and work 3 rnds following Chart A.

Set up color pats: Work Chart B over 36 sts, pm, rep Chart B 12 times over the rem 144 sts.

Continuing charted pats as established, work 30 rnds of Chart C twice, then Rnds 1–29.

Work 3 rnds following Chart A, break CC.

TOP EDGE

With MC, knit 2 rnds.

Drawstring Eyelet rnd: K17, k2tog, yo, knit to end.

Knit 3 rnds.

Turning rnd: Purl.

FACING

Option 1:

Knit 6 rnds.

Fold facing to WS, enclosing drawstring with both ends coming out of drawstring eyelet, and whip st live sts to inside of bag. Pull both ends of drawstring through toggle and cinch closed.

Option 2: Make another hole for inserting the straps as follows:

Knit 2 rnds.

Next rnd: K10, BO 14 sts, knit to end.

Next rnd: K10, CO 14 sts, knit to end.

Knit 2 rnds.

Place sts on yarn holder. The facing will be folded and secured after the straps are attached.

Finishing
Block bag.

EMBROIDERY
Chain st along the center branches of the star as shown in photo. Use the lazy-daisy stitch to make a flower in the center of each star. Place 2 French knots at the ends of each branch.

STRAPS (make 2)
Option 1: Sew leather straps to bag at center bottom back and top front of bag.

Option 2:
Cut fabric straps 3" x 40". Using a ¼" seam allowance, sew zipper to edge of strap, leaving 2" at each end. Fold selvage edges over ¼", then fold entire strap in half to cover zipper tape. Sew together. Attach braid by topstitching onto strap. Attach bottom of strap to bag by threading end into hole at bottom of bag and sewing. Attach top of strap to bag by inserting straps into hole at top of bag and sewing.

I-CORD
With dpns, CO 4 sts.

Row 1: K4; do not turn; slide sts to opposite end of needle.

Rep Row 1 until I-cord measures 4".

BO and secure end of yarn.

Attach I-cord to top edge of bag over center back, "trapping" straps under the I-cord when attaching.

LINING
Cut one piece of black wool fabric 5 ½" x 9 ½" for bottom of bag and another piece 15 ½" x 30 ½" for sides. Fold side piece in half and sew with ¼" seam allowance to make tube. Sew bottom piece to side tube, clipping corners to allow proper fit. Place inside-out lining into knit bag and sew in along facing edge. Fold facing over raw edges of the lining (enclosing drawstring with both ends coming out of drawstring eyelet), and sew to lining. Pull both ends of drawstring through toggle and cinch closed.

Close up of knapsack embroidery

Mother and daughter on the road, Rauland, Telemark, Norway, 1890s.
GAUSTA COLLECTION, VESTERHEIM ARCHIVE

CHART B: CENTRAL PANEL

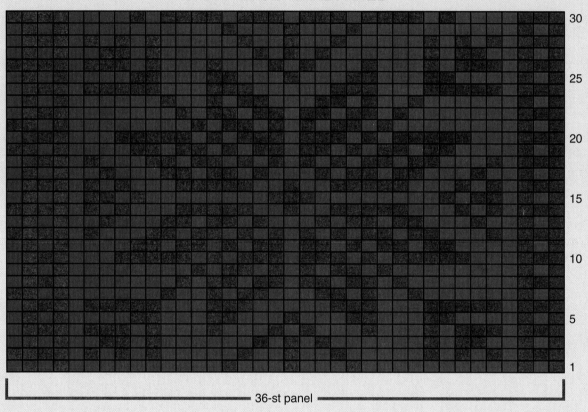

30

25

20

15

10

5

1

36-st panel

CHART A

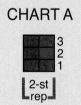

3
2
1

2-st
rep

CHART C: MAIN FABRIC

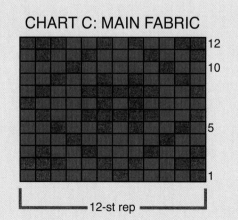

12

10

5

1

12-st rep

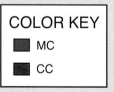

COLOR KEY

MC

CC

Kumihimo

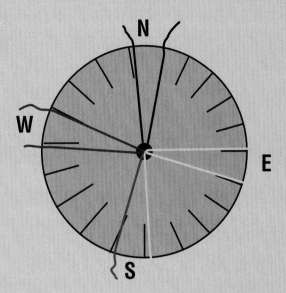

*K*umihimo is a Japanese braiding technique called "The Gathering of Threads."
We discovered this braid in a Norwegian braid
book and discovered that it is relatively easy
to make and creates a sturdy drawstring for the
knapsack. These directions are for an eight-
strand braid.

Step 1: Prepare Template

Cut a 5" circle out of a cereal box using a
coffee can lid as a template. Poke a hole through the
center of the circle with a pencil. Cut at least 14 slits
½" deep evenly spaced around the outside edges of
the circle. The number of slits and spacing between
them is not critical.

Step 2: Set Up Template

Cut two 72" lengths each of 3 colors as
desired (black, red, and white are used here).
Cut one 72" length each of 2 colors as desired
(gold and green are used here). Tie all the strands
together and slip knot through hole in the center

of template. Hold the template in right hand and
think of it as a compass—the section pointing
away from you is north, the section pointing toward you is south, the section on the right side
is east, and the section on the left side is west.
Set up the threads by hooking them into a slot in the
following layout: a pair of two black threads each in
its own slot in the north section, two white threads
each in its own slot on the east side, one gold and
one green thread in separate slots on the south section, and two red threads in separate slots in the
west section.

Step 3: Weaving Pattern

*Take the left thread from the south section
(green here) and bring it up and place in slot
to the left of both north threads. Take the right
thread from the north section and bring it down
and place it in a slot to the right of the south
thread. Rotate the template a quarter turn (90
degrees) counterclockwise; rep from * until you
have the desired length of cord. Tie ends together
when finished.

Dancing Hat

This traditional hat was made for a man named Oddgeir, who was a member of a traditional Norwegian dancing troupe. It was knit by his mother from what she had on hand, because the cream color appears to be knit in a cotton thread, providing an interesting contrast to the wool used for the rest of the hat. The new hat differs from the original in the hem treatment—the original was topstitched in a Bargello style of stitching, while the new version has a knitted-in color hem in the flavor of the original. We think Oddgeir's mother would have approved. While knitting this hat, try daydreaming about traditional Nordic dancing, and you might find your feet tapping in time to your needles!

Size
Woman's average

Finished Measurements
Circumference at head: Approx. 22"
Length (not including pom-pom): Approx. 14"

Materials

- Reynolds *Whiskey* (100% Shetland wool; 195 yds/50g per ball): 1 ball each Navy #3608 (MC), Gold #101 (A), Acid Green #103 (B), Red #011 (C), Mushroom #031 (D), and Dark Green #059 (E)
- Size 1 (2.25mm) double-pointed needles (set of 5) and two 16" circular needles or size needed to obtain gauge
- Small crochet hook
- Stitch markers, 1 in CC for beg of rnd
- Tapestry needle
- Pom-pom maker (optional)

Gauge
35 sts and 37 rnds = 4" (10cm) in stranded St st.
Adjust needle size as necessary to obtain correct gauge.

Special Technique
Provisional Cast-On: With crochet hook and waste yarn, make a chain several sts longer than desired cast-on. With knitting needle and project yarn, pick up indicated number of sts in the "bumps" on back of chain. When indicated in pattern, "unzip" the crochet chain to free live sts.

Pattern Notes

- Change to double-pointed needles when stitches no longer fit comfortably on circular needle.
- Take care with tension when working stranded stockinette stitch; if necessary, change to smaller needle size when working plain stockinette stitch to match gauge of color pattern sections.

Instructions

BORDER AND HEM

With circular needle and MC, using provisional method, CO 192 sts; pm for beg of rnd and join, taking care not to twist sts.

Knit 8 rnds.

Turning rnd: Purl.

Work 8 rnds following Bargello chart.

Remove provisional cast-on and place live sts on 2nd circular needle; fold work along turning rnd so that needles are parallel.

Joining rnd: Using the needle in front and MC, *insert right tip into first st on front needle, then into first st on back needle and knit them tog; rep from * around—192 sts.

BODY OF HAT

Knit 1 rnd and inc 6 st evenly around—198 sts.

Work even in St st for 2 ¼".

Work 37 rnds following Grand Star Chart.

Next rnd (dec): With MC, *k31, k2tog; rep from * around—192 sts.

Knit 1 rnd, placing markers every 24 sts.

Dec rnd: *Knit to 2 sts before marker, k2tog; rep from * around—184 sts.

Cont in St st and rep Dec rnd [every other rnd] 5 times—144 sts.

Knit 1 rnd, removing markers.

Work 27 rnds following North Star Chart.

With MC, knit 1 rnd, placing markers every 24 sts.

Cont in St st and work Dec rnd on next, then [every other rnd] 7 times—96 sts.

Knit 1 rnd, removing markers.

Next rnd: [K14, k2tog] twice, k30, [k2tog, k14] twice, k2—92 sts.

Knit 1 rnd.

Work 9 rnds following Little Dipper Chart.

Change to MC and knit 1 rnd.

Next rnd: Knit and dec 2 sts evenly around, placing markers every 15 sts—90 sts.

Work Dec rnd on next, then [every other rnd] 10 times—24 sts.

Knit 1 rnd, removing markers.

Break yarn, leaving a 10" tail; thread tail through rem sts, pull tight, then secure to WS.

OLD NORWEGIAN RECIPE

KRUMKAKE

I STARTED MAKING *KRUMKAKE* AFTER PURCHASING AN OLD NORDIC WARE STOVE-TOP *KRUMKAKE* IRON AT A GARAGE SALE. HAVING NEVER MADE *KRUMKAKE*, I RECRUITED MY GOOD FRIEND KIRSTEN LANGSTEMO TO TEACH ME THE TRICKS TO MAKING PERFECT *KRUMKAKE*. IT TOOK US A FEW BATCHES TO GET THE RECIPE JUST RIGHT, BUT WE FINALLY GOT THE PERFECT BLEND OF BATTER AND FOUND THE IDEAL IRON TEMPERATURE. ONCE WE GOT GOING, THERE WAS NO VISITING—JUST SERIOUS SPOONING, SQUEEZING, COUNTING, FLIPPING, REMOVING, AND ROLLING. IT WAS FAST-PACED AND WE CRANKED OUT HUNDREDS OF *KRUMKAKE*. WE LIKE TO EAT THEM PLAIN OR FILLED WITH WHIPPED CREAM—THIS IS A GREAT HOLIDAY TREAT.

2 EGGS
1 c. GRANULATED SUGAR
½ c. SOFT BUTTER
1 TSP. CARDAMOM, FRESHLY GROUND
1 ½ c. FLOUR
1 c. MILK

BEAT EGGS WELL; ADD SUGAR, BUTTER, AND CARDAMOM. BEAT. ADD FLOUR AND MILK AND MIX UNTIL SMOOTH.

PLACE IRON DIRECTLY OVER MEDIUM HEAT ON TOP OF STOVE. HEAT BOTH SIDES OF IRON BY FLIPPING OVER. IRON IS HOT ENOUGH WHEN WATER SPRINKLED ON INSIDE SIZZLES. PLACE 1 LEVEL TABLESPOON OF BATTER IN CENTER OF PREHEATED *KRUMKAKE* IRON. CLOSE LID AND SQUEEZE HANDLES TOGETHER. (IF BATTER OOZES OUT ALONG EDGES, SCRAPE OFF EXCESS BATTER AND USE LESS BATTER FOR NEXT ONE.) COOK UNTIL LOWER SIDE OF COOKIE IS LIGHT BROWN, ABOUT 1 TO 2 MINUTES, FLIP IRON AND COOK FOR AN ADDITIONAL 30 SECONDS. REMOVE COOKIE FROM IRON WITH A SPATULA. IMMEDIATELY FORM INTO CONE SHAPE WHILE STILL HOT. THE CONE CAN BE SHAPED OVER A METAL OR WOODEN FORM AND SLIPPED OFF THE END WHEN COOLED.

Finishing

Weave in all ends.   Block to finished measurements.

POM-POM

Use pom-pom maker or follow instructions as follows:
Cut 2 cardboard circles the size of desired pom-pom. Cut a hole in the center of each circle, approx ½" in diameter. Thread a tapestry needle with 1 very long strand each of all colors. Holding both circles together, insert needle through center hole, over the outside edge, through center again, going around and around until entire circle is covered and center hole is filled (thread more length of yarn as needed). With sharp scissors, cut yarn between the 2 circles all around the circumference. Using 2 [12"] strands of yarn (tying ends), wrap yarn between circles, going 2 or 3 times around; pull tight and tie into a firm knot. Remove cardboard and fluff out pom-pom. Trim ends as necessary to make pom-pom circular. Attach pom-pom to hat using tying ends.

The original hat was worn by Oddgeir Fletre, immigrant from Hardanger, Norway, when dancing with Leikarringen Heimhug in Chicago in the 1950s.

Dancers at the Norse-American Centennial held at the Minnesota State Fairgrounds, June 6–9, 1925.
NORSE-AMERICAN CENTENNIAL COLLECTION, VESTERHEIM ARCHIVE

LITTLE DIPPER

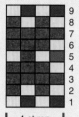

9
8
7
6
5
4
3
2
1

└ 4-st rep ┘

BARGELLO BAND

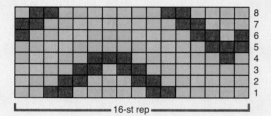

8
7
6
5
4
3
2
1

├─ 16-st rep ─┤

NORTH STAR

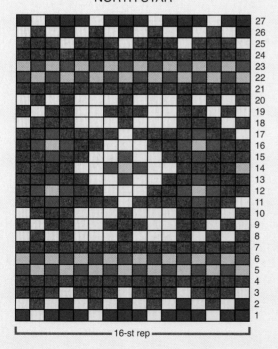

27
26
25
24
23
22
21
20
19
18
17
16
15
14
13
12
11
10
9
8
7
6
5
4
3
2
1

├─ 16-st rep ─┤

GRAND STAR

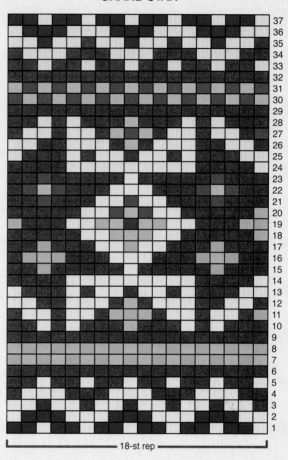

37
36
35
34
33
32
31
30
29
28
27
26
25
24
23
22
21
20
19
18
17
16
15
14
13
12
11
10
9
8
7
6
5
4
3
2
1

├─ 18-st rep ─┤

COLOR KEY

 Navy (MC)

 Gold (A)

 Acid Green (B)

 Red (C)

 Mushroom (D)

 Dark Green (E)

Dancing Mittens

Size
Woman's average

Finished Measurement
Circumference around hand: 7 ½"

Materials

- Reynolds *Whiskey* (100% Shetland wool; 195 yds/50g per ball): 1 ball each Navy #3608 (MC), Gold #101 (A), Acid Green #103 (B), Red #011 (C), Mushroom #031 (D), and Dark Green #059 (E) *(see Pattern Notes)*
- Size 1 (2.25mm) double-pointed needles (set of 5) or size needed to obtain gauge
- Stitch markers, 1 in CC for beg of rnd
- Tapestry needle

Gauge
35 sts and 37 rnds = 4" (10cm) in stranded St st.
Adjust needle size as necessary to obtain correct gauge.

Just like the Dancing Hat, these mittens will make you want to dance—or at the very least, they will make you long for the first cold days of the season so you have an excuse to wear them. These mitts are perfect for that late fall walk, when you find yourself kicking the leaves in your path and thinking wistfully about the snow to come. Two-color knitting has never looked so good!

Special Abbreviations
M1L (Make 1 Left): Insert LH needle from front to back under the running thread between the last st worked and next st on LH needle; knit into the back of resulting loop.
M1R (Make 1 Right): Insert LH needle from back to front under the running thread between the last st worked and next st on LH needle. With RH needle, knit into the front of resulting loop.

Pattern Notes
- If you are working the hat and mittens as a set, purchase 2 balls each of Navy (MC) and Red (C); 1 ball each of the other colors is enough to make both hat and mittens.
- Take care with tension when working stranded stockinette stitch; if necessary, change to smaller needle size when working plain stockinette stitch to match gauge of color pattern sections.

Instructions

CUFF
With MC, CO 64 sts; distribute evenly on 4 dpns, pm for beg of rnd and join, taking care not to twist sts.
Work k2, p2 Rib for 3".

THUMB GUSSET

Setup rnd: K32, pm, k2, pm, knit to end of rnd.

Inc rnd: Knit to marker, slip marker, M1R, knit to next marker, M1L, slip marker, knit to end of rnd—66 sts.

Cont in St st and rep Inc rnd [every other rnd] 11 times—88 sts with 26 sts between markers.

Knit 1 rnd.

Next rnd: Knit to marker, CO 2 sts, place the 26 sts for thumb on waste yarn, knit to end—64 sts.

HAND

Work 27 rnds following North Star Chart *(see Dancing Hat, page 77)*. With MC, work even in St st until mitten reaches tip of pinkie and on last rnd, place markers every 8 sts.

TOP

Dec rnd: *Knit to 2 sts before marker, k2tog; rep from * around—56 sts.

Cont in St st and rep Dec rnd [every other rnd] 6 times—8 sts.

Break yarn, leaving a 5" tail.

Using tapestry needle, thread tail through rem sts, pull tight, and secure on WS.

THUMB

Distributing sts evenly on 4 dpns, slip 26 thumb gusset sts back to dpns, with MC, pick up and knit 6 sts at thumb opening, pm for beg of rnd—32 sts.

Work even in St st until thumb measures 2 ¾".

Dec rnd: *K2, k2tog; rep from * around—24 sts.

Work 2 rnds even.

Dec rnd: *K1, k2tog; rep from * around—16 sts.

Work 1 rnd even.

Dec rnd: K2tog around—8 sts.

Break yarn, leaving 6" tail.

With tapestry needle, thread yarn through rem sts and pull tight; secure tail on WS.

Finishing

Weave in all ends.

Block to finished measurements.

Brothers Paul and Harold Rosendahl admiring a snowwoman, Houston County, Minnesota, 1910s.
ROSENDAHL COLLECTION,
VESTERHEIM ARCHIVE

Sami Sweater

Sizes

Adult's small (medium, large, X-large, XX-large)
Instructions are given for smallest size, with larger sizes in parentheses. When only 1 number is given, it applies to all sizes.

Finished Measurements

Chest: 36 ¾ (41, 43 ¾, 48, 52 ¼)"
Length: 24 (26, 27, 28, 29)"
Sleeve length: 17 ½ (18, 18 ½, 19, 19 ½)"

Materials

- Reynolds *Lite Lopi* (100% Icelandic wool; 109 yds/50g per skein): 10 (12, 14, 16, 18) skeins Natural White #0051 (MC); 2 skeins Red #0414 (A); 1 (2, 2, 2, 2) skein(s) Yellow #0435 (B); 2 skeins Blue #0442 (C)
- Size 8 (5mm) double-pointed needles (set of 5) and 24" circular needles or size needed to obtain gauge
- Size 9 (5.5mm) 24" circular needle
- Size I/9 (5.5) crochet hook
- Stitch markers
- Waste yarn
- Tapestry needle

Gauge

17 sts and 26 rnds = 4" (10cm) in St st with smaller needles.
Adjust needle size as necessary to obtain correct gauge.

The image of the Sami people in colorful costumes herding reindeer is reflected in this sweater. Simple edging and patterns in the traditional Sami colors of red, blue, yellow, and off-white surround a plain background. The edges and triangle patterns are worked in garter stitch, which add depth to the simple design. The original child's Sami dress that inspired this sweater and the matching mittens has limited history. It was knit in Norway around the 1940s by an unknown relative and was donated to Vesterheim in 1989.

Special Techniques

Crochet Picot Cast-On: See page 92.
3-Needle Bind-Off: With RS tog and needles parallel, using a 3rd needle, knit tog a st from the front needle with 1 from the back. *Knit tog a st from the front and back needles, and slip the first st over the 2nd to bind off. Rep from * across, then fasten off last st.

Pattern Notes

- The sweater is knit in the round to the armholes, then divided into front and back, which are worked back and forth separately.
- The sleeves are picked up and knit from the top down; they are worked back and forth for the first 8 rows, then in the round to the cuff.
- The picot edging at hem is made with a crochet picot cast-on; the edging at cuffs and around hood is made with a crochet picot bind-off. The picot edging may be omitted if making the sweater for a male.
- The hood is knit onto the garment starting at the center back. The shaped back of the hood is worked first, then the sides of hood are created by picking up stitches around the back of hood. These sides are worked back and forth and, at the same time, are attached to the side back neck stitches. Finally, patterned hood trim and neck placket are worked.

Sami-style dress, knit in Norway by a relative, ca. 1940.

Instructions

BODY

With crochet hook, larger circular needle, and A, using crochet picot CO method, CO 130 (145, 155, 170, 185) sts as follows: *crochet CO 3, chain 3, join loop; rep from *, crochet CO 0 (0, 1, 1, 1), then place loop from crochet hook onto needle for last st; pm for beg of rnd and join, taking care not to twist sts.

Work 16-rnd Body Bottom Chart, and on Rnd 11, change to larger needle and inc as indicated—156 (174, 186, 204, 222) sts.

With MC only, knit every rnd until piece measures 14 ½ (15 ½, 16, 16, 16 ½)", ending last rnd 4 sts before beg of rnd marker.

Split for armholes

Next rnd: Removing marker, k8 and put on waste yarn for underarm; k69 (79, 85, 93, 103) sts and put on waste yarn for front; k8 and put on waste yarn for underarm, k71 (79, 85, 95, 103) sts and leave on needle for back.

Back

Work even in St st until armhole measures 7 ½ (8 ½, 9, 10, 10 ½)", ending with a WS row.

Shoulder Trim

Work 16 rows following Back Shoulder Chart, beg and end where indicated for size being worked.

Break A, leaving a very long tail to be used later for shoulder join; place sts on waste yarn for holder.

Front

Slip k69 (79, 85, 93, 103) front sts to needle and join yarn ready to work WS row.

With MC, work even in St st for 12 rows, ending with RS row.

Next row (WS): P26 (31, 33, 37, 41), pm, p17 (17, 19, 19, 21), pm, p26 (31, 33, 37, 41).

Inset trim

Setup row (RS): Slipping markers, with MC, knit to marker; join C and work Front Inset Chart to next marker, beg and end where indicated for size being worked; with MC, knit to end.

Next 7 rows: Continue working St st with MC on left and right sides and chart pat in center between markers.

Place sts for center neck and right front on separate pieces of waste yarn for holders—26 (31, 33, 37, 41) sts rem for left front.

Left Front

Work 2 rows in St st.

Dec row (RS): Knit to last 3 sts, k2tog, k1—25 (30, 32, 36, 40) sts. Cont in St st and rep Dec row [every 4 rows] 5 (6, 6, 7, 8) times—20 (24, 26, 29, 32) sts.

Work even until armhole measures 7 ½ (8 ½, 9, 10, 10 ½)", ending with a WS row.

Work 16 rows following Left Front Shoulder Chart.

Slip 20 (24, 26, 29, 32) right back shoulder sts to smaller dpn; join right front and back shoulder sts using 3-needle BO.

Right Front

Slip right front sts to needle, ready to work RS row; join MC.

Work 2 rows in St st.

Dec row (RS): K1, ssk, knit to end—25 (30, 32, 36, 40) sts. Cont in St st and rep Dec row [every 4 rows] 5 (6, 6, 7, 8) times—20 (24, 26, 29, 32) sts.

Work even until armhole measures 7 ½ (8 ½, 9, 10, 10 ½)", ending with a WS row.

Work 16 rows following Right Front Shoulder Chart.

Slip 20 (24, 26, 29, 32) left back shoulder sts to smaller dpn; join right front and back shoulder sts using 3-needle BO.

31 (31, 33, 37, 29) sts rem on waste yarn for back neck.

SLEEVES

Slip 8 underarm sts to dpn.

With RS facing, using smaller circular needle and A, pick up and knit 78 (90, 96, 102, 108) sts around armhole, turn.

Work Rows 1–8 following Top Sleeve Chart as follows: Join first underarm st to first sleeve st with an ssk, knit to end of row, turn. Do not turn at end of Row 8; there will still be 78 (90, 96, 102, 108) sleeve sts after all underarm sts have been joined at end of Row 8; pm for beg of rnd and join.

Cont in the rnd and complete Top Sleeve Chart.

Break C and cont with MC.

Shape Sleeve

Dec rnd: K1, ssk, knit to last 2 sts, k2tog—76 (88, 94, 100, 106) sts. Rep Dec rnd [every 6 rnds] 12 (0, 0, 0, 0) times, then [every 5 rnds] 2 (8, 12, 3, 5) times, and [every 4 rnds] 0 (12, 8, 20, 18) times—48 (48, 54, 54, 60) sts.

Work even until sleeve measures 15 ½ (16, 16 ½, 17, 17 ½)" from pickup rnd or until 2" short of desired length.

Work 16 rnds following Cuff Chart.

Work crochet picot BO as follows: With crochet hook in right hand and needle in left hand, *use crochet hook to BO 3, chain 3; rep from * around.

Break yarn and secure end.

HOOD

Hood Back

Place the center 11 sts of the 31 (31, 33, 37, 39) sts back neck sts on needle—10 (10, 12, 16, 18) sts rem on separate holders on each side of center back neck sts.

Row 1 (RS): With MC, k1, *M1, k1; rep from * to end—21 sts.

Row 2: Sl 1, purl to end.

Row 3: Sl 1, knit to end.

Rep Rows 2 and 3 until hood measures 2 ½", ending with a WS row.

Inc row (RS): Sl 1, k1, M1, knit to last st, M1, k1—23 sts.

Slipping first st of every row and working in St st, rep Inc row [every RS row] 7 times—37 sts.

Slipping first st of every row, work even until hood measures 7 ½", ending with a WS row.

Dec row (RS): Sl 1, ssk, knit to last 3 sts, k2tog, k1—35 sts.

Slipping first st of every row, rep Dec row [every RS row] 8 times, ending with Dec row, do not turn after last row—19 sts.

Hood Sides

Slip 10 (10, 12, 16, 18) left and right back neck sts to separate dpns.

Row 1 (RS): With MC, pick up and knit a total of 41 (40, 41, 40, 41) sts along the left side of hood and for last st of the total, ssk it tog with first back neck st on dpn; turn.

Row 2: Purl to end of live sts, pick up and purl a total of 41 (40, 41, 40, 41) sts along right side of hood and for last st, p2tog with first back neck st on dpn; turn—101 (99, 101, 99, 101) sts.

Row 3: Sl 1, knit to last st, ssk with next back neck st.

Row 4: Sl 1, purl to last st, p2tog with next back neck st.

Rep Rows 3 and 4 until all back neck sts have been joined with hood sts, ending with a RS row; do not turn after last row—101 (99, 101, 99, 101) sts.

FRONT PLACKET

Slip 17 center front neck sts to dpn.

Row 1 (RS): With MC, pick up and knit a total of 28 (32, 34, 38, 40) sts along the left side of front placket and for last st, ssk it tog with first st on dpn holding center front sts; turn.

Row 2: Sl 1, purl to end of live sts, pick up and purl a total of 28 (32, 34, 38, 40) sts along right side of placket and for last st, p2tog with first st on dpn holding center front sts; turn—157 (163, 169, 175, 181) sts.

Norwegian Sami family outside a lavu (tent), ca. 1900. VESTERHEIM ARCHIVE

OLD NORWEGIAN RECIPE
LUTEFISK

THIS IS THE SPACE WHERE A RECIPE FOR LUTEFISK WOULD HAVE APPEARED, BUT WE COULDN'T BRING OURSELVES TO ACTUALLY INCLUDE IT. IF YOU'RE HUNGRY FOR LUTEFISK, IT'S BEST TO FIND YOUR LOCAL LUTHERAN CHURCH AND WATCH FOR THEIR LUTEFISK MEAL, WHICH IS INEVITABLY JUST AROUND THE CORNER.

Row 3: Join C and work Hood Chart along edge of hood, slipping first st as before and joining last st with next center front st. Cont working chart, slipping first st of each row and joining last st of each row with next center front st until all the center front sts are joined.
Work crochet picot BO as for sleeve cuff.

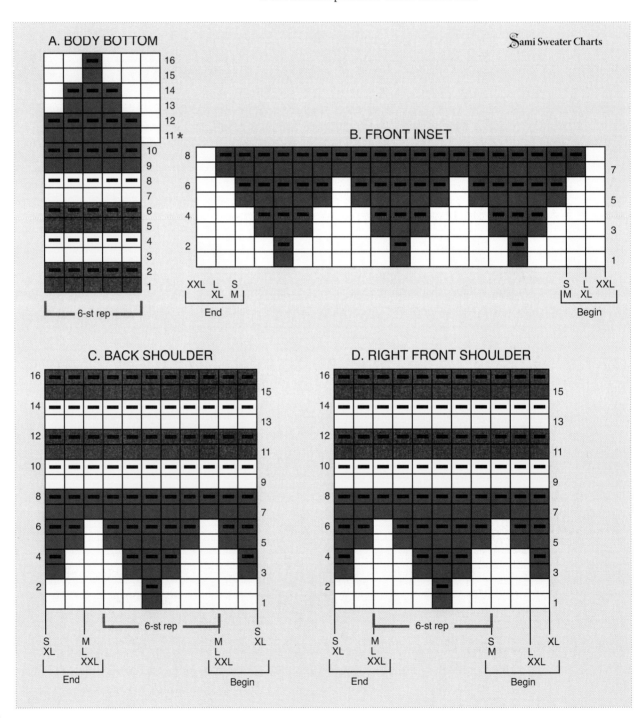

A. BODY BOTTOM

Sami Sweater Charts

B. FRONT INSET

C. BACK SHOULDER

D. RIGHT FRONT SHOULDER

Finishing

Weave in all ends.

Block to finished measurements.

With 2 strands each of all 4 colors, work fishtail braid 64" long, or to desired length.

Weave braid in and out of eyelets on hood.

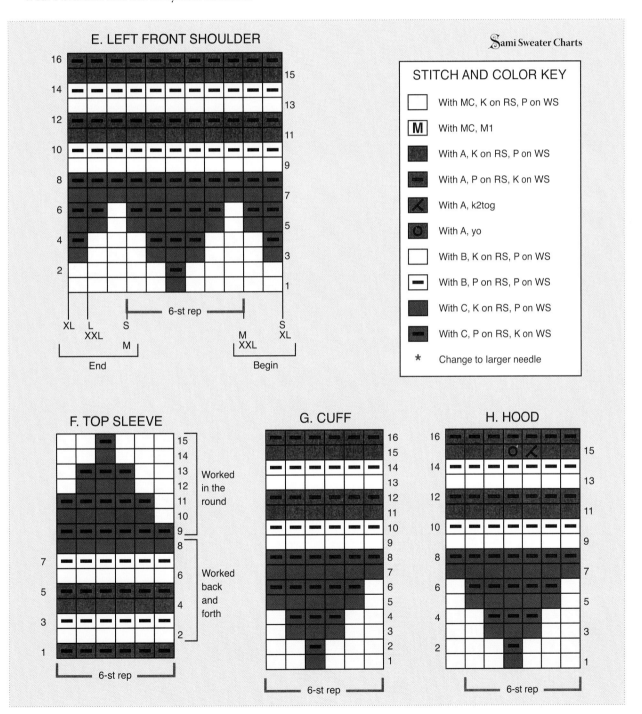

STITCH AND COLOR KEY

☐	With MC, K on RS, P on WS
M	With MC, M1
■	With A, K on RS, P on WS
▬	With A, P on RS, K on WS
✗	With A, k2tog
⊙	With A, yo
☐	With B, K on RS, P on WS
▬	With B, P on RS, P on WS
■	With C, K on RS, P on WS
▬	With C, P on RS, K on WS
*	Change to larger needle

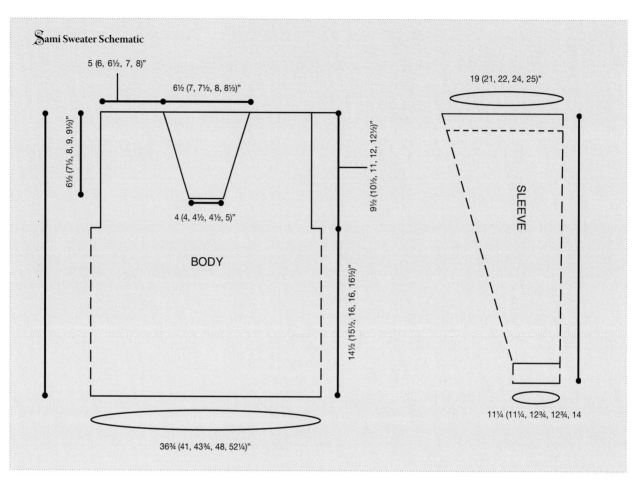

Sami Sweater Schematic

5 (6, 6½, 7, 8)"

6½ (7, 7½, 8, 8½)"

6½ (7½, 8, 9, 9½)"

9½ (10½, 11, 12, 12½)"

4 (4, 4½, 4½, 5)"

BODY

14½ (15½, 16, 16, 16½)"

36¾ (41, 43¾, 48, 52¼)"

19 (21, 22, 24, 25)"

SLEEVE

11¼ (11¼, 12¾, 12¾, 14

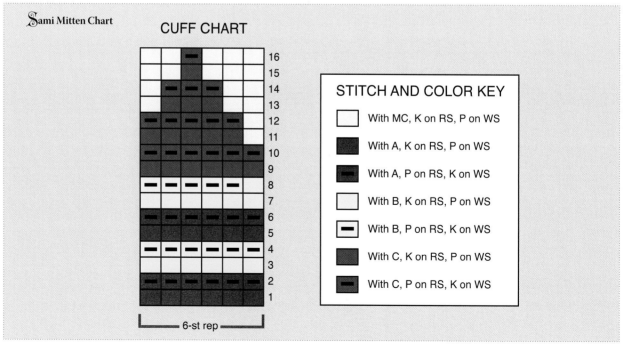

Sami Mitten Chart

CUFF CHART

16
15
14
13
12
11
10
9
8
7
6
5
4
3
2
1

6-st rep

STITCH AND COLOR KEY

With MC, K on RS, P on WS

With A, K on RS, P on WS

With A, P on RS, K on WS

With B, K on RS, P on WS

With B, P on RS, K on WS

With C, K on RS, P on WS

With C, P on RS, K on WS

86

Fish Tail Braid

Cut 8 lengths of yarn (2 of each color). Measure the yarn 3 times longer than desired finished cord. Lay strands out as illustrated—follow this color pattern: red, blue, yellow, cream, cream, yellow, blue, red.

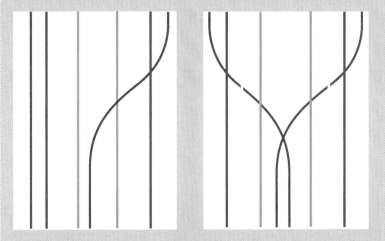

Step 1: Bring the outer right red strand to center.

Step 2: Bring the outer left red strand to center, crossing over Step 1 strand.

Step 3: Bring the outer right blue strand to center, crossing over red strands.

Step 4: Bring the outer left blue strand to center, crossing over the red and blue strands.

Step 5: Bring the outer right yellow strand to center, crossing over the previously moved strands.

Step 6: Bring the outer left yellow strand to center, crossing over the red, blue, and yellow strands.

Step 7: Bring the outer right cream strand to center, crossing over previously moved strands.

Step 8: Bring the outer left cream strand to center, crossing over the previously moved strands.

Continue to follow the pattern as established by crossing the outmost strand over to the center until desired length. Tie knot and thread through eyelet openings in hood and/or mitten cuff.

Sami Mittens

Size
Adult average

Finished Measurements
Length: 12"
Palm Circumference: 9"

Materials

- Reynolds *Lite Lopi* (100% Icelandic wool; 109 yds/50g per skein): 2 skeins Natural White #0051 (MC), 1 skein each Red #0414 (A), Yellow #0435 (B), and Blue #0442 (C)
- Size 5 (3.75mm) double-pointed needles (set of 4 or 5)
- Size 7 (4.5mm) double-pointed needles (set of 4 or 5) or size needed to obtain gauge
- Size G/7 (4.5mm) crochet hook
- Tapestry needle

Gauge
16 sts and 26 rnds = 4" (10cm) in St st with larger dpns and 2 strands of yarn held tog.
Adjust needle size as necessary to obtain correct gauge.

Felt balls, Sami Mittens

The Sami Mittens were designed to match the sweater, but they work great as a stand-alone project as well. The mittens are very easy to knit and feature the fishtail braid and felted ball embellishments.

Special Techniques
Crochet Picot Cast-On: See page 92.
Fishtail Braid: See page 87.
Felt Balls: See page 31-32.

Pattern Notes
- Crochet picot cast-on is used to make the picot edging at cuff (see page 92).
- The hand of the mittens is knit with the yarn doubled for a warmer mitten.
- Left and Right Mittens are the same.

Instructions

GAUNTLET CUFF
With crochet hook, larger dpn, and A, and using crochet picot method, CO 36 sts as follows: crochet CO 2 sts, *chain 3 loops, join loop, crochet CO 3 sts; rep from * 10 times; place loop from crochet hook onto dpn for last st. Distribute sts evenly on 3 or 4 dpns, pm for

beg of rnd and join, taking care not to twist sts.

Work 16-rnd Cuff Chart (see pg 86); break C.

With MC, knit 9 rnds.

Eyelet rnd: Change to smaller dpns; *ssk, yo, k1, p1; rep from * around.

Work 6 rnds in k1, p1 Rib.

Add 2nd strand of MC, change to larger dpns, and knit 2 rnds.

THUMB GUSSET

Rnd 1: K18, pm, M1, k1, M1, pm, k17—38 sts.

Rnds 2 and 3: Knit.

Rnd 4 (inc): Knit to marker, slip marker, M1, knit to marker, M1, slip marker, knit to end—40 sts.

Rep [Rnds 2–4] 3 times, then work Rnds 2–3 once more—46 sts.

Next rnd: Removing markers, knit to marker, place 11 thumb gusset sts on waste yarn for holder, CO 1 st over gap, k17—36 sts.

MAIN MITTEN

Knit every rnd for approx 3" or until mitten reaches ½" below tip of little finger; dec 1 st on last rnd—35 sts.

Top Decrease

Rnd 1: *K3, k2tog; rep from * around—28 sts.

Rnd 2 and all even rnds: Knit.

Rnd 3: *K2, k2tog; rep from * around—21 sts.

Rnd 5: *K1, k2tog, rep from * around—14 sts.

Rnd 7: K2tog around—7 sts.

Break yarn leaving a 6" tail.

With tapestry needle, thread tail through rem sts, pull tight, and secure end to WS.

THUMB

Place 11 thumb gusset sts back on dpns; with yarn doubled, pick up and knit 4 sts along main mitten join—15 sts.

Knit every rnd until thumb is ½" from tip of thumb.

Work top dec as for top of mitten.

Finishing

Weave in ends.

Block.

Make 2 fishtail braids approx 22" long.

Thread through Eyelet rnd with ends at outside edge of mitten (see photo).

Make 2 felted balls each with A, B, and C.

Sew 3 balls (1 in each color) to point where braid emerges from mitten (see photo).

OLD NORWEGIAN RECIPE

NORWEGIAN-STYLE KRINGLE

WHEN MY MOTHER MADE THIS RECIPE, SHE ALWAYS INSISTED THAT WE NEEDED TO FINISH IT ON THE DAY IT WAS BAKED, CLAIMING THAT IT WAS "NO GOOD AS DAY-OLD." IMAGINE BEING TOLD TO HAVE SECONDS OF DESSERT!

½ c. UNSALTED BUTTER, SLICED
1 c. ALL-PURPOSE FLOUR
PINCH OF SALT
2–4 TBSP. ICE WATER
1 c. MILK
½ c. BUTTER, SOFTENED
1 c. FLOUR
3 TBSP. GRANULATED SUGAR
½ TSP. PURE ALMOND EXTRACT
3 EGGS
1 ½ c. SIFTED CONFECTIONERS' SUGAR
1 ½ TSP. VANILLA EXTRACT
2 TBSP. UNSALTED BUTTER, SOFTENED
1 TBSP. MILK
¾ c. SLIVERED ALMONDS

HEAT OVEN TO 375° F.

TO MAKE THE PASTRY, CUT THE SLICED STICK OF UNSALTED BUTTER INTO 1 c. FLOUR UNTIL THE MIXTURE LOOKS PEBBLY. USE A FORK TO STIR IN A PINCH OF SALT AND THE ICE WATER UNTIL THE MIX IS A SOFT DOUGH. FORM THE DOUGH INTO TWO 14 X 3-INCH RECTANGLES ON AN UNGREASED COOKIE SHEET, BY PRESSING IT INTO PAN WITH FINGERS. SET ASIDE.

TO MAKE THE FILLING, HEAT MILK AND BUTTER IN A MEDIUM SAUCEPAN UNTIL BOILING; REMOVE FROM HEAT. TO THE MILK AND BUTTER, ADD 1 c. FLOUR AND STIR UNTIL SMOOTH. BEAT THE SUGAR INTO MIXTURE, THEN ADD EGGS ONE AT A TIME INTO THE FLOUR-MILK MIXTURE. ADD ALMOND EXTRACT AND BEAT WELL. SPREAD THIS MIXTURE OVER THE TWO BOTTOM LAYERS. BAKE FOR 15–20 MINUTES OR UNTIL LIGHTLY BROWNED

WHILE KRINGLE IS BAKING, PREPARE GLAZE: COMBINE THE CONFECTIONERS' SUGAR, VANILLA EXTRACT, BUTTER, AND MILK. DRIZZLE GLAZE OVER THE STILL-WARM KRINGLE AND SET ASIDE. SPRINKLE ALMONDS OVER THE TOP OF THE KRINGLE WHILE THE GLAZE IS STILL TACKY.

Flower Hat with Earflaps

Size
Woman's average

Finished Measurements
Circumference: 20"
Length (including earflaps): 12"

Materials

- Dale of Norway *Falk* (100% superwash wool; 116 yds/50g per ball): 1 ball each Cocoa (MC) and Turquoise (CC)
- Size 4 (3.5mm) double-pointed needles (set of 5) and 16" circular needles or size needed to obtain gauge
- Size E/4 (3.5mm) or F/5 (3.75mm) crochet hook
- Stitch markers, 1 in CC for beg of rnd
- Tapestry needle

Gauge
24 sts and 30 rnds = 4" (10cm) in stranded 2-color St st.
Adjust needle size as necessary to obtain correct gauge.

The flower motif on this hat was inspired by a pair of mittens that featured an unusual mix of a flower pattern and a snowflake pattern. It is interesting to note that what most of us refer to as a traditional Norwegian snowflake design was intended to represent a flower. The original mittens were knit by an immigrant's mother in 1911. The name of the immigrant and the mother are unknown, since the mitten came to Vesterheim by way of an antique dealer. The mittens are from the Sunnfjord region of Norway, which is north of Bergen.

Pattern Notes
- Crochet picot cast-on is used to make the picot edging at the cuff; crochet picot bind-off is used the make the edging around the earflaps (see Crochet Picot Cast-On sidebar on page 17).
- The color pattern is worked using the "stranded" method, i.e., by carrying both colors at once. Avoid long floats on the inside of the hat in those areas where more than five consecutive stitches are worked in one color by catching the color not in use with the working color.
- Decreases are worked within the two-color pattern and are indicated on the charts.
- Change to dpns when stitches no longer fit comfortably on the circular needle.
- Earflaps are worked separately and sewn on.

Instructions
EDGING
With circular needle and CC, CO 120 sts using the crochet picot

method as follows: crochet CO 2 sts, *chain 3 sts to make picot loop, join loop, crochet CO 3 sts over needle; rep from * (119 sts), end with [chain 3, join loop, place loop from crochet hook onto needle] for the last st, pm for beg of rnd and join, taking care not to twist sts.

Rnd 1: (CC) Purl.

Rnd 2: Join MC and knit.

Rnd 3: (MC) Purl.

Rnds 4 and 6: (CC) Knit.

Rnds 5 and 7: (CC) Purl.

Rnd 8: (MC) Knit and place markers every 20 sts.

BODY

Work 20 rnds of Chart A and on last rnd, work color pat and dec as follows: *k5, ssk, k5, k2tog, k6; rep from * around—108 sts.

Work 13 rnds of Chart B and on last rnd, work color pat and dec as follows: *k3, ssk, k7, k2tog, k4; rep from * around—96 sts.

Work 12 rnds of Chart C and on Rnd 9, work color pat and dec as follows: *k2, ssk, k7, k2tog, k3; rep from * around; break off CC after chart is complete—84 sts.

CROWN

Dec rnd: With MC, *ssk, knit to 3 sts from marker, ktog, k1; rep from * around—72 sts.

Continue in St st and rep Dec rnd [every other rnd] 4 times, ending with Dec rnd—24 sts.

Break yarn, leaving 6" tail.

With tapestry needle, thread yarn through rem sts, and pull tight; secure tail on WS.

EARFLAP (make 2)

With dpns and MC, CO 17 sts.

Work 18 rows of Earflap Chart, working decs on Rows 14 and 16 as follows: working in color pat, k1, ssk, work to last 3 sts, k2tog, k1.

Slip rem 13 sts to holder.

Earflap Edging

With RS facing and using CC, pick up and knit 12 sts along one edge of earflap, k13 sts from holder, pick up and knit another 12 sts along other edge.

Knit 1 row with CC, then knit 2 rows MC, and 2 rows CC.

With CC, work crochet picot BO as follows: With crochet hook in right hand and needle in left hand, use crochet hook to BO 1 st, *chain 3, join loop by working sc into last st on needle; BO 3; rep from * around.

Break yarn, leaving a 15" tail.

Pull yarn through rem st.

With tapestry needle and tail, sew earflap to hat.

Finishing

Weave in loose ends. Block to finished measurements.

These mittens were made by an immigrant's mother in 1911 before the immigrant left Sunnfjord (north of Bergen) for Minnesota. Unfortunately, the name and gender of the wearer are unknown because the mitten came by way of an antique dealer. The mittens are made of handspun wool.

CHART C

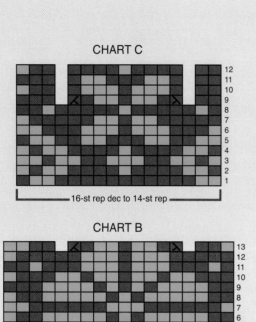

16-st rep dec to 14-st rep

EARFLAP CHART

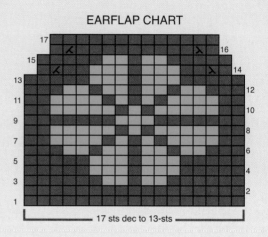

17 sts dec to 13-sts

CHART B

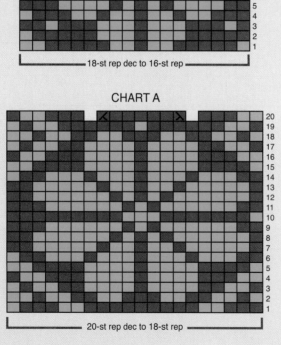

18-st rep dec to 16-st rep

STITCH AND COLOR KEY

With MC, k on RS, p on WS.

With CC, k on RS, p on WS.

With MC, ssk.

With MC, k2tog.

CHART A

20-st rep dec to 18-st rep

Flower Mittens

Size
Woman's average

Finished Measurements
Circumference: 8 ½"
Length: 11"

Materials

- Dale of Norway *Falk* (100% superwash wool; 116 yds/50g per ball): 1 ball each Cocoa #3072 (MC) and Turquoise #6027 (CC)
- Size 4 (3.5mm) double-pointed needles (set of 5) or size needed to obtain gauge
- Stitch markers, 1 in CC for beg of rnd
- Tapestry needle

Gauge
24 sts and 30 rnds = 4" (10cm) in stranded 2-color St st.
Adjust needle size as necessary to obtain correct gauge.

Knit a pair of mittens featuring the same flower and snowflake motif as the earflap hat. The original mittens were made of hand-spun wool.

Special Abbreviation
S2KP2: Slip 2 sts tog knitwise, k1, pass the slipped sts over; this is a centered double decrease.

Pattern Notes
- After working the cuff, follow the appropriate color charts throughout and shape as indicated.
- The color pattern is worked using the "stranded" method, i.e., by carrying both colors at once. Avoid long floats on the inside of the mitten in those areas where more than 5 consecutive stitches

are worked in one color by catching the color not in use with the working color.

- The main chart shows the left-hand mitten; to make a right-hand mitten, work Rnds 1–11 of the Right Palm Chart (below the main chart), then continue with the main chart.

Instructions

LEFT MITTEN

Cuff

With MC, CO 44 sts and distribute evenly on 4 dpns; pm for beg of rnd and join, taking care not to twist sts.

Work 12 rnds of k1, p1 Rib.

Join CC and continuing in est rib, work stripes as follows: 1 rnd CC, 1 rnd MC, 1 rnd CC, 2 rnds MC, 2 rnds CC, 2 rnds MC, 1 rnd CC, 1 rnd MC, 1 rnd CC [break CC], 6 rnds MC.

Thumb Gusset

Setup rnd: With MC, k40, pm, k3, pm, k1.

Rnd 1: Join CC and beg Mitten Chart.

Rnds 2, 4, 6, 8 (inc): Knit to marker, slip marker, M1, knit to marker, M1, slip marker, k1—2 sts inc'd each rnd, with 11 sts between markers on Rnd 8.

Rnd 3 and all odd rnds: Work even.

Rnd 10: Knit to marker, remove markers, and slip 11 sts between markers to waste yarn or holder, CO 11 sts *in pat* to create thumb opening, knit to end of rnd—52 sts.

Main Mitten

Work even for 28 rnds and on last rnd, place marker after 26th st.

Top Decrease

Dec rnd: *K1, ssk, work to 2 sts before marker, k2tog, rep from * once—48 sts.

Rep Dec rnd [every rnd] 10 more times—8 sts.

Next rnd: [K1, S2KP2] twice—4 sts.

Break yarn, leaving 6" tails.

With tapestry needle, thread yarn through rem sts, and pull tight; secure tails on WS.

Thumb

Slip 11 thumb gusset sts back to needle; with MC, pick up 13 sts around the thumb opening, pm for beg of rnd—24 sts.

Join CC and work Thumb Chart for 17 rnds, placing marker after 12th st on last rnd.

Dec rnd: *K1, ssk, knit to 2 sts before marker, k2tog, rep from * around—20 sts.

Rep Dec rnd [every rnd] 3 more times—8 sts.

Next rnd: [K1, S2KP2] twice—4 sts.

Break yarn, leaving 6" tails.

Ingeborg Gausta Bruflodt (Herbjørn Gausta's sister) spinning, Fillmore County, Minnesota, early 1900s.

GAUSTA COLLECTION,
VESTERHEIM ARCHIVE

With tapestry needle, thread yarn through rem sts, and pull tight; secure tails on WS.

RIGHT MITTEN

Work cuff as for Left Mitten.

Thumb Gusset
Setup rnd: With MC, k28, pm, k3, pm, k13.
Work as for Right Mitten but follow Left Palm Chart for thumb gusset.
When finished with thumb gusset, complete as for Right Mitten.

Finishing

Weave in ends and block as necessary.

People on a hillside, probably Sigdal, Norway, 1890s. GAUSTA COLLECTION, VESTERHEIM ARCHIVE

MITTEN CHARTS

Flower Mitten Charts

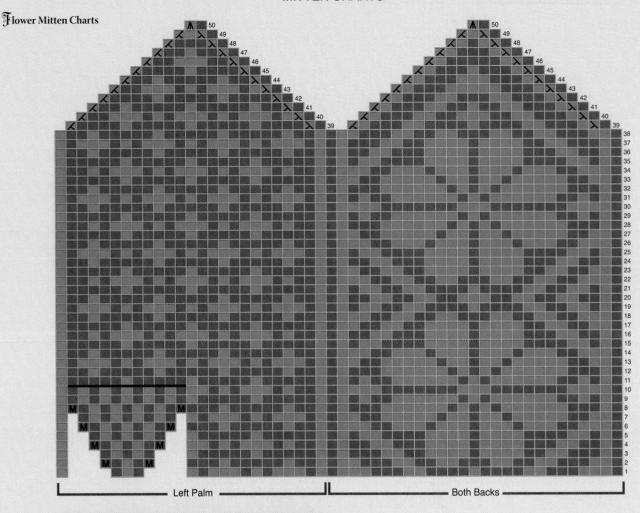

Left Palm ————— Both Backs

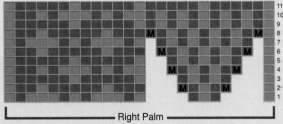

Right Palm

THUMB CHART

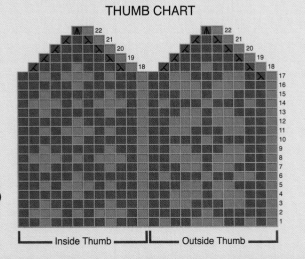

Inside Thumb ——— Outside Thumb

96

STITCH AND COLOR KEY

- ▢ K with MC
- ▢ K with CC
- ■ No Stitch
- **M** M1 with MC
- ⟍ Ssk with CC
- ⟍ Ssk with MC
- ⟋ K2tog with CC
- ⟋ K2tog with MC
- ⋀ S2KP2 with CC
- ⋀ S2K2P with MC
- — Put 11 sts on holder, then CO 11

Crochet Picot Cast-On

(for Sami Sweater and Flower Hat)

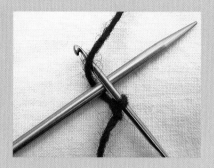

Step 1:
First Cast-On Stitch: Make a slipknot on the crochet hook. Hold the needle in the LEFT hand and the crochet hook in the RIGHT hand. With the yarn under the needle, wrap the yarn under the needle and clockwise around the crochet hook as shown. Pull the yarn through the slipknot.

Step 2:
2nd (and Following) Cast-On Stitches: Bring the yarn back under the needle, wrap the yarn as before and pull it through the loop on the hook.

Step 3:
Make the Picot Loop: With crochet hook, make 3 "freestanding" chain sts.

Step 4:
Close the Picot Loop: Single crochet through the bottom of the last cast-on st on the needle (i.e., the one that was made in Step 2).

Step 5:
Repeat a pattern of cast on 3 sts (as in Step 2) and chain 3 sts and secure (as in Steps 3 and 4) until you have cast on 1 st short of the desired total number of sts.

Step 6:
Final Stitch: For the last st, bring yarn in back; slip the loop from the crochet hook onto the needle as shown.

"Mitten Day" Mittens

Size
Child's average

Finished Measurements
Circumference: 7 ½"
Length: 9"

Materials

- Blackberry Ridge *Mer-Made DK Weight* (100% superwash merino wool; 260 yds/114g [4 oz.] per skein)
  Girl's version: 1 skein each Cream (MC) and Black (CC)
  Boy's version: 1 skein each Black (MC) and Cream (CC)
- Size 4 (3.5mm) double-pointed needles (set of 5) or size needed to obtain gauge
- Stitch markers, 1 in CC for beg of rnd
- Tapestry needle

Gauge
24 sts and 30 rnds = 4" (10cm) in stranded 2-color St st.
Adjust needle size as necessary to obtain correct gauge.

The tradition of unpacking the family mittens on October 14 dates back to the Middle Ages, when time was tracked using a wooden calendar stick. Since Sue's birthday is also October 14, we wanted to design a special set of mittens that anyone would be proud to unpack for the upcoming winter months.

The inspiration for the mittens was two contrasting pairs of red and black mittens that were made in the 1930s for a boy and a girl. Elements of both pairs were used in creating the updated version—the snowflake from the boy's mittens and the palm pattern from the girl's mittens. Also, the girl's mittens traditionally featured a lace pattern in the cuff while the boy's mittens used k1, p1 ribbing. To make the set more interesting, they are worked in positive and negative by reversing the main color and the contrasting color. The original mittens had characters on the thumbs, and we thought they were a nice touch, so we worked them into this pattern as well. It is interesting to note that the boy motif is upside down on the original mittens, while the girl's is right side up. The originals were donated to Vesterheim by Helga Lund Algyer in 1972.

Pattern Notes
- After working the cuff, follow the appropriate charts throughout and shape as indicated.
- The colorwork is done using the "stranded" method, carrying both colors at once. Avoid long floats on the inside of the mitten in those areas where more than 5 consecutive stitches are worked in one color by catching the color not in use with the working color.

- The directions are written for both the girl's and boy's versions of the mittens. Note that the cuffs, small charts, and thumbs are different for each version. The main mitten is the same for either version, but the background and contrasting colors are reversed.
- The main chart shows the left-hand mitten; to make a right-hand mitten, mark the thumb gusset before working the palm pattern in the Setup Rnd, then work the Right Palm Chart.

Instructions

LEFT MITTEN

Cuff

With dpns and MC, CO 40 sts; place marker and join, taking care not to twist sts.

Girl's version

Rnd 1: *K1, yo, S2KP2, k3, yo; rep from * around.

Rnd 2: Knit.

Rep Rnds 1 and 2 in the following stripe pattern: 6 total rnds MC, 1 rnd CC, 2 rnds MC, 2 rnds CC, 2 rnds MC, 1 rnd CC, 6 rnds MC.

Boy's version

Rnds 1–20: Work 20 rnds of k1, p1 Rib in the same stripe pattern as the girl's version.

Both versions

Work 9-rnd Cuff Chart (different for each version).

Thumb Gusset

Setup rnd: With MC, k34, pm, k5, pm, k1.

Join CC and follow Left Mitten Chart.

Rnds 3, 5, 7 (inc): Following chart, knit to gusset marker, slip marker, M1, knit to marker, M1, slip marker, k1—11 gusset sts between markers after last inc rnd.

Rnd 8: Knit to marker, remove markers, and slip 11 sts between markers to waste yarn or holder; CO 11 sts *in pat* to create thumb opening—46 sts.

Main Mitten

Work even following chart through Rnd 36, and on last rnd, pm between back hand and palm sts.

Top Mitten

Dec rnd: Cont to follow chart; *k1, ssk, knit to 2 sts before marker, k2tog; rep from * once more—42 sts.

Cont to follow chart and rep Dec rnd [every rnd] 9 times—8 sts.

Next Rnd: [K1, S2KP2] twice—4 sts.

Break yarn, leaving 6" tails.

With tapestry needle, thread yarn through rem sts, and pull tight; secure tails on WS.

Thumb

Slip 11 thumb gusset sts back to needle; with MC, pick up and knit 13 sts around the rem thumb opening—24 sts.

Set of mittens made in the 1930s for a boy and girl. The originals were donated to Vesterheim by Helga Lund Algyer in 1972.

Attach CC; follow Thumb Chart for either girl's or boy's version through Rnd 12 and on last rnd, pm between front and back thumb sections.

Dec rnd: Cont to follow Thumb Chart; *k1, ssk, knit to 2 sts before marker, k2tog; rep from * once more—20 sts.

Cont to follow chart and work Dec rnd [every rnd] 3 times—8 sts.

Next Rnd: [K1, S2KP2] twice—4 sts.

Break yarn leaving 6" tails.

With tapestry needle, thread yarn through rem sts, and pull tight; secure tails on WS.

RIGHT MITTEN

Work cuff as for Left Mitten.

Thumb Gusset

Setup rnd: With MC, k24, pm, k5, pm, k11.

Work as for Left Mitten but follow Right Palm Chart for thumb gusset.

When finished with thumb gusset, complete as for Left Mitten.

Finishing

Weave in tails. Block.

This Calendar stick (or primstav), dated 1566, is from the Jørstadmoen farm in Gudbrandsdal. This was among the gifts sent from Norwegian museums to (Vesterheim and the) Norwegians in America in 1925 in honor of 100 years of emigration.

Mitten Day

by Kate Martinson

The ancient Nordic people used a lunar calendar to divide the year into two half-year portions. Summer began on April 14 and winter on October 14. The tracking of the days was done using a long, wooden two-sided calendar stick. This stick, which Norwegians called a *primstav,* had a series of carved notches that represented individual days of ancient significance, and eventually, days of observation of Christian ritual. The use of the *primstav* in Norway appears to have begun in the later Middle Ages and continued until the 1700s. On the summer side of the calendar stick, a treelike symbol was carved on the top of the stick to mark the first day of summer. Conversely, an incised carving of a mitten symbolizing the beginning of winter marked the top of the winter side of the stick.

According to the *primstav,* October 14 was the day winter began. The mitten was the perfect symbol to mark this day in a land so far north. The mitten is the article of clothing that allows real work to be done outside during the long, inhospitable winter season. To the ancient Nordic peoples, winter was a powerful season. In fact, they calculated age not by counting anniversaries, but by counting the winters a person had endured.

Although the calendar stick has been replaced by printed almanacs or calendars, many Scandinavians still use October 14 to symbolize the start of winter, and this is the day they get out the heavy clothes and begin to make final winter preparations.

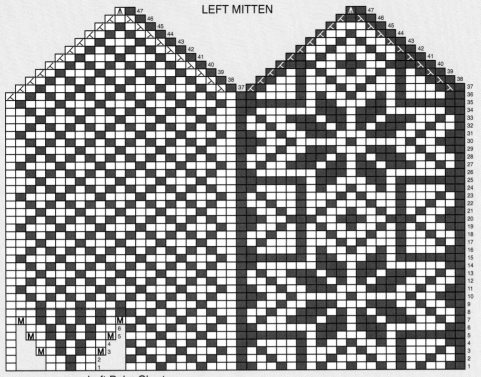

Left Palm Chart

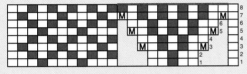

Right Palm Chart

THUMB CHART (Girl's)

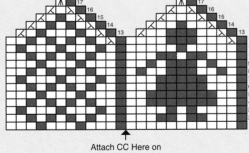

CUFF CHART(Girl's)

Attach CC Here on
1st rnd of thumb

STITCH AND COLOR KEY

☐ K with MC (see Note)

■ K with CC (see Note)

☐ No Stitch

⊟ Purl

Ⓜ M1

⧄ Ssk

⧅ K2tog

⋏ S2KP2

— Put 11 sts on holder,
then CO 11 in pattern

Note: Main Mitten and Palm Charts are the
same for both versions, and are shown with
Girl's version of MC/CC; reverse MC/CC for
Boy's version.

Thumb and Cuff charts different for each
version and are shown with correct MC/CC
for version being worked.

THUMB CHART (Boy's)
(shown in Boy's MC/CC)

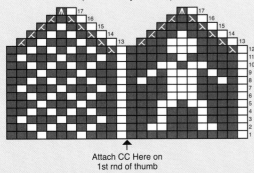

CUFF CHART
(Boy's)
(shown in Boy's MC/CC)

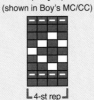

Attach CC Here on
1st rnd of thumb

101

Portrait of an Immigrant: Christie Sleen Tillotson

Anna Christina Tillotson in a Voss folk costume, Boone County, Illinois, 1890s.

Christie Sleen, the original owner of the Voss headscarf, died in 1923, just five days before her seventy-seventh birthday. Christie is remembered as a deeply religious woman with a heart of gold. Along with her church and local charities, she generously supported a retirement home and an orphanage in her childhood home of Vossestrand, Norway.

Christie was born in 1846 to an unwed mother and the local schoolmaster in Vossestrand, north of Voss in western Norway. In 1866, she immigrated as a single woman to the Jefferson Prairie Settlement in northern Illinois, where she worked as a housekeeper for Ole Tillotson, a widower with eight children. She married Ole in 1868 and had nine children with him. Her youngest child was Dena Bertina, the headscarf donor's grandmother. Christie was a firm believer in higher education, and a number of her children attended college.

One of her grandsons remembers Christie as a proud woman who did not like people criticizing her for driving a horse and buggy at a time when she could easily afford to own and drive a car. She secretly purchased a new Cadillac, learned how to drive it, and showed up at church one Sunday behind the wheel. People were astounded. After that maiden voyage, she parked the car in the garage and resumed using her horse and buggy. Apparently, she never drove the Cadillac again.

Another grandson, who grew up on the farm, remembers Christie taking him in the buggy to collect rent and mortgage payments from families who had borrowed money, owed rent, or were buying property from Christie. They went from house to house conducting their business. After each stop, Christie would tuck the payments in special pockets in her petticoats. When they returned home, she had several hundred dollars rustling in her slip!

Christie's youngest daughter, Dena, married Robert Hanold and had three children. Dena died of a ruptured appendix at age thirty, leaving behind a seven-year-old daughter, a five-year-old son, and a twenty-two-month-old son, Terrance Hanold. The daughter was sent to live with a relative, and Robert did his best to raise the two boys. When Terrance was about ten years old, he went to live on the eighty-acre family farm in Manchester Township, Boone County, Illinois, where he also attended carpenter school. For Terrance, the happiest years of his youth were spent living with his Aunt Anna and Uncle Ed Iverson.

Terrance went on to college, became a lawyer, married, and had children, one of which is Ruth Hanold Crane. Ruth is the generous donor of the Voss headscarves.

The original headscarf was discovered in an immigrant trunk in the attic of the old farmhouse that Terrance inherited when his Aunt Anna passed away. Ruth believes that the headscarf belonged to Christie or her mother. Ruth's own interest in the headscarf was piqued in the 1980s when she began making her own Voss *bunad* and headscarf. Ruth donated the headscarf she stitched herself, once again reviving the traditional pattern.

Voss Family Sweaters

Adult Voss Sweaters, front

The two-color stranded ski sweater that we typically think of as traditional Norwegian knitting is a relatively recent addition to the textile heritage of Norway. Depending upon the region, color-knit garments did not come into fashion until the mid- to late 1800s. This sweater design was inspired by the Voss headscarf, which was discovered in an old immigrant's trunk that was packed away in a farmhouse attic. We also took note of and incorporated the tradition of making the background of a man's sweater dark with a light-colored foreground. As expected, the woman's is the opposite, with a light background and dark foreground.

Adult Voss Sweaters

Size(s)

Adult's X-small (small, medium, large, X-large, XX-large) Instructions are given for smallest size, with larger sizes in parentheses. When only 1 number is given, it applies to all sizes.

Materials

- Cascade *220* (100% wool; 220 yds/100g per skein)
  Man's version: 3 (4, 4, 5, 5, 6) skeins Brown #7822 (MC), 3 (3, 4, 4, 5, 5) skeins Green Heather #9460 (A), and 1 skein Forest #9429 (B)
  Woman's version: 3 (4, 4, 5, 5, 6) skeins Green Heather #9460 (MC), 3 (3, 4, 4, 5, 5) skeins Brown #7822 (A), and 1 skein Plum #7807 (B)
- Size 5 (3.75mm) double-pointed needles (set of 5), 16" and 24" circular needles
- Size 7 (4.5mm) double-pointed needles (set of 5) and 24" circular needles or size needle to obtain gauge
- Tapestry needle
- Cotton waste yarn
- Stitch markers, 1 in CC for beg of rnd

Gauge

20 sts and 24 rnds = 4" (10cm) in stranded 2-color St st.
Adjust needle size as necessary to obtain correct gauge.

Finished Measurements

Chest: 38 ¾ (42, 45¼, 48½, 51½, 54¾)"
Body Length: 25¼ (26¾, 27¼, 28¼, 28¾, 29¼)"
Sleeve Length to Underarm: 19½ (19½, 20½, 20½, 21½)"

Pattern Stitch

Corrugated Ribbing (multiple of 4 sts)
Rnd 1: *K2 MC, p2 B; rep from * around.
Rep Rnd 1 for pat.

Special Techniques

3-Needle Bind-Off: With RS tog and needles parallel, using a 3rd needle, knit tog a st from the front needle with 1 from the back. *Knit tog a st from the front and back needles, and sl the first st over the 2nd to bind off. Rep from * across, then fasten off last st.
Sewing and Cutting Steeks: See sidebar on page 107.

Pattern Notes

- The body of the sweater is worked in the round from the bottom up. After knitting, the armhole positions are marked, reinforced by machine sewing, then cut. This is called "steeking" *(see sidebar)*.
- The neck opening is also formed using a sew-and-cut method.
- The Body Chart shows only the right half of the body front; the left half is worked as a mirror image of the charted pattern. Note that the center stitch of the front, shown on the chart at the left edge and bordered in red, should *not* be repeated when repeating the pattern for the left half of the front. After working the mirror image for the left side, repeat the chart for both halves of the back.

- The Sleeve Chart shows only the right half of the sleeve; the left half is worked as a mirror image of the charted pattern. The center stitch of the sleeve, shown on the chart at the left edge and bordered in red, should *not* be repeated when repeating the pattern for the left half of the sleeve.
- The sweater includes an optional diamond pattern in the lower right corner. There are some design options provided, or you can design your personal design, such as initials, using the blank diamond outline provided. Substitute Diamond Chart for Body Chart in area where you desire to place diamond.
- When working sleeve, switch to 16" circular needle when there are enough stitches to do so.

Close up of Voss sweater motif

Instructions

BODY

With smaller circular needle and B, CO 180 (192, 204, 216, 232, 244) sts; pm for beg of rnd and join, taking care not to twist sts.

Join A and work 2" in corrugated ribbing. Break B.

Inc rnd: Change to larger needle, join MC, and knit, increasing 14 (18, 22, 26, 26, 30) sts evenly around—194 (210, 226, 242, 258, 274) sts.

Next rnd: Knit with MC.

Next rnd (beg Band pat): *Beg at point designated for the size you are working, work 97 (105, 113, 121, 129, 137) sts in stranded 2-color St st across Rnd 1 of Band Chart, pm for side edge; rep from * for back.

Complete 29-rnd Band Chart.

Work Body Chart, beginning at the st and rnd indicated on chart for size you are working.

Place sts (including side st markers) on waste yarn to hold for sewing armholes and neck opening.

SLEEVE

With smaller dpns and B, CO 40 (40, 44, 48, 52, 52) sts, pm for beg of rnd and join, taking care not to twist sts.

Join A and work 2" in corrugated ribbing. Break B.

Inc rnd: Change to larger dpns, join MC, and knit, increasing 11 (13, 13, 15, 15, 17) sts evenly around—51 (53, 57, 63, 67, 69) sts.

Next rnd: Knit with MC.

Work Rnds 1–4 of Sleeve Chart, beg where indicated for size being worked.

Inc rnd: Cont in established pat, k1, M1, knit to end of rnd, M1—53 (55, 59, 65, 69, 71) sts.

Cont working Sleeve Chart and rep Inc rnd [every 4 rnds] 21 (22, 23, 24, 24, 24) times more—95 (99, 105, 113 117, 119) sts.

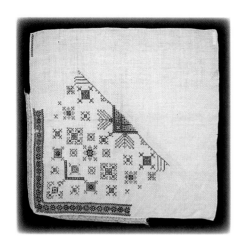

This skaut, or headscarf, was probably made and worn by Ingeborg Larsdatter Lillethun of Vossestrand, Norway. Ingeborg immigrated in 1891 to Boone County, Illinois. She died in 1909.

Detail of Voss headscarf

Work even until sleeve measures 19½ (19½, 20½, 20½, 21½)" or desired length.

FACING

Beg working back and forth in rev St st with MC. *(See Alphabet sidebar on page 114 for directions on placing a secret message in the facing.)*

Row 1 (RS): Purl.

Row 2: K1, M1, knit to last st, M1, k1—97 (101, 107, 115, 119, 121) sts.

Row 3: P1, M1, purl to last st, M1, p1—99 (103, 109, 117, 121, 123) sts.

Rep [Rows 2 and 3] twice more—107 (111, 117, 125, 129, 131) sts.

Place sts on waste yarn for holder.

Weave in ends.

Block to finished measurements.

CUT ARMHOLES

Mark armhole depth below markers indicating sides of body. Using a contrasting piece of cotton yarn, baste a line from side marker to marked armhole depth position, going between 2 center side edge sts. *(See Marking, Sewing, and Cutting a Steek for Sleeves sidebar).*

After sewing in sleeves, loosely sew live sts of facing to WS of armhole, covering cut edge.

NECKLINE MARK AND SEW

On front of sweater, mark off 31 (33, 37, 40, 43, 45) sts on each side of neck for shoulders. Slip rem 35 (39, 39, 41, 43, 47) sts to separate holder for neck. Mark neck depth of 3 (3, 3 ½, 3 ½, 3 ½, 4)" at center front. Using a piece of cotton yarn, baste the shape of neckline around front of sweater. With machine, sew along the marked neck 2 times and cut out crescent, leaving ¾" seam allowance.

SHOULDER JOIN

Join shoulder seams using 3-needle BO.

NECK EDGING

With smaller 16" circular needle, pick up and knit 112 (112, 116, 116, 116, 120) sts around neck as follows: *2A, 2B; rep from * around. Work 7 rnds in corrugated rib. Break A.

FACING

Rnd 1: With B, knit.

Rnd 2: Purl.

Rnds 3–8: *K2, p2; rep from * around.

Fold facing to WS and secure by loosely sewing live sts to pickup rnd on the inside.

Finishing

Weave in all ends.

Block to finished measurements.

Marking, Sewing and Cutting
a Steek for Sleeves

Marking Armhole

Cutting Armhole

Step 1: Measure the diameter of the sleeve at the turning ridge before the facing. Mark the armhole depth on the body based on this measurement. Use a contrasting piece of cotton yarn to baste a line between the two center underarm stitches from the side marker (still on the needle) to the bottom of the armhole; make sure to clearly mark the bottom of the armhole. This basting yarn will be your cutting line.

Step 2: Thread the sewing machine with a contrasting thread and set the machine to small stitches. Place the knitting under the machine foot and begin to sew, slowly moving the basted armhole forward; do not allow the fabric to pucker. Stitch on top of the knitted stitches *adjacent to* the basting yarn, going from the shoulder to the bottom of the armhole; turn, sew across bottom stitches of the armhole, then sew back up on the top of the knitted stitches *adjacent to* the other side of the basting thread. You should have a long, narrow "U" machine-stitched around the basting yarn. Try to avoid sewing in the "ditch," or over the bars between the stitches, since this does not catch enough of the fiber for a strong steek.

NOTE: Some knitters prefer to sew the shoulder seam together at this point to prepare the garment for sewing in the sleeves. This will minimize any extra handling of the garment once the sleeve opening is cut. The raw stitches will be exposed for a shorter time than if the shoulder seam is joined after the cutting.

Step 3: Cut along the basting yarn to open up the armhole. Sew the sleeve into place 1–2 stitches from the cut edge on each side, attaching the sleeve along the first row of the facing.

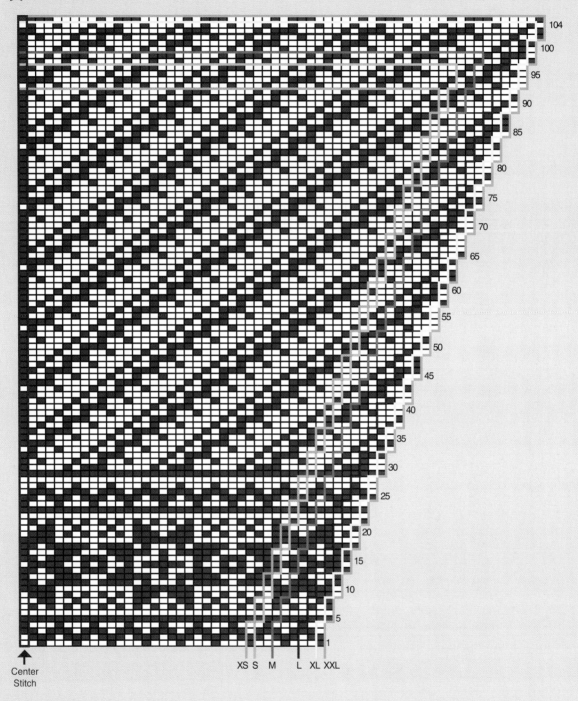

Center
Stitch

XS S   M   L   XL XXL

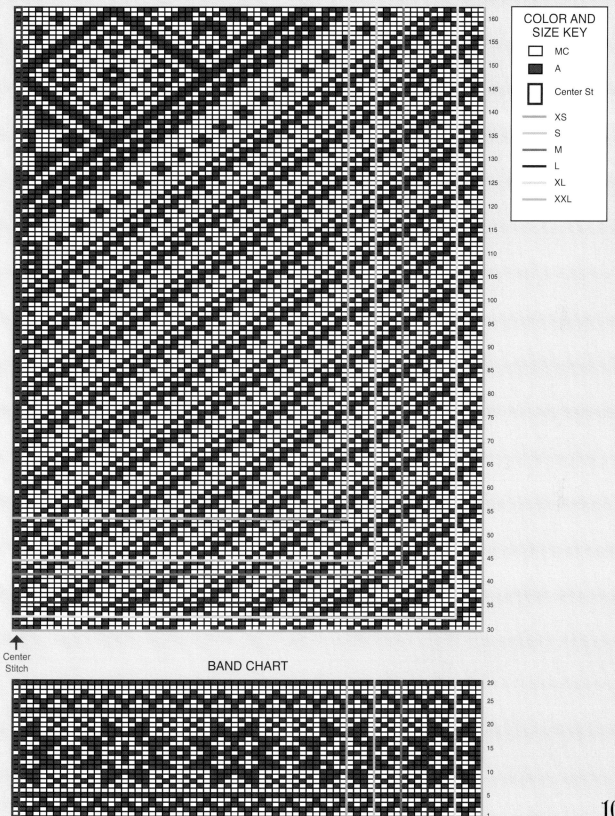

COLOR AND
SIZE KEY

☐ MC

■ A

☐ Center St

—— XS

—— S

—— M

—— L

—— XL

—— XXL

Center
Stitch

BAND CHART

XS   S   M   L   XL   XXL

Center
Stitch

Family Voss: Optional Diamond insets

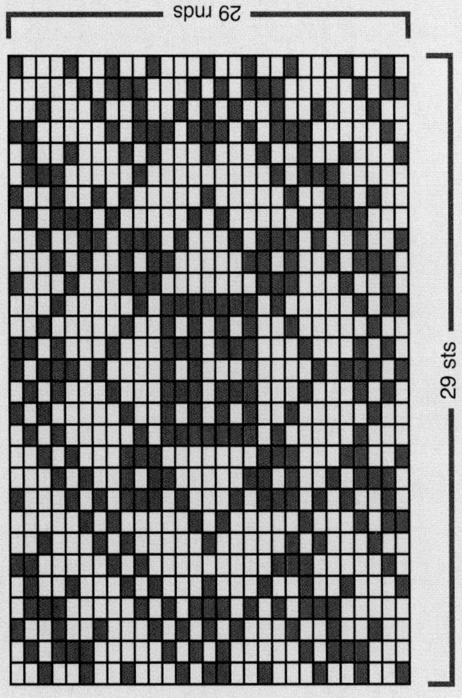
29 rnds
29 sts

Option A

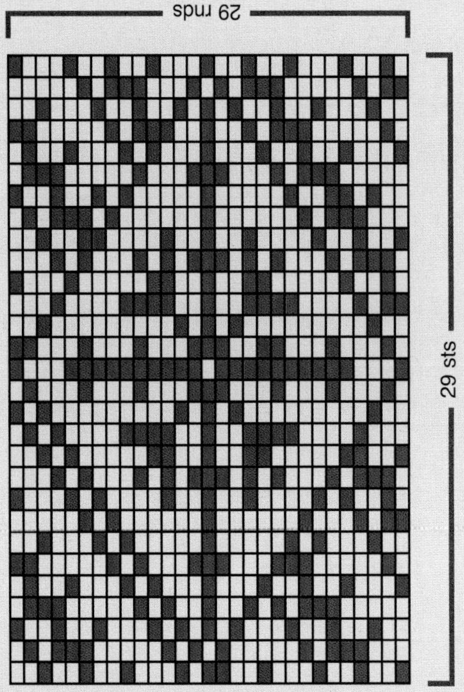
29 rnds
29 sts

Option B

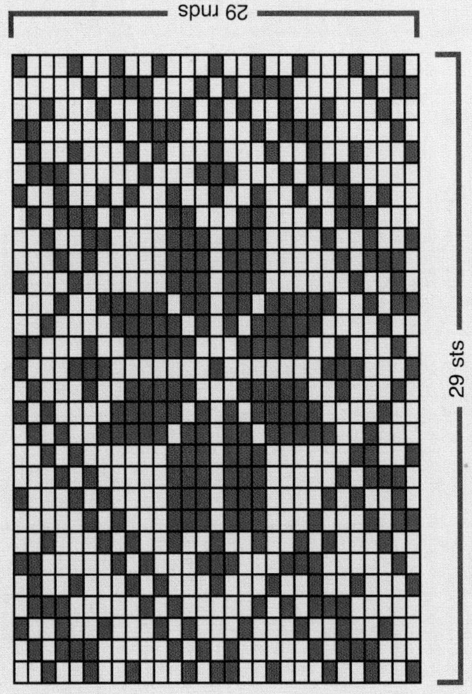
29 rnds
29 sts

Option C

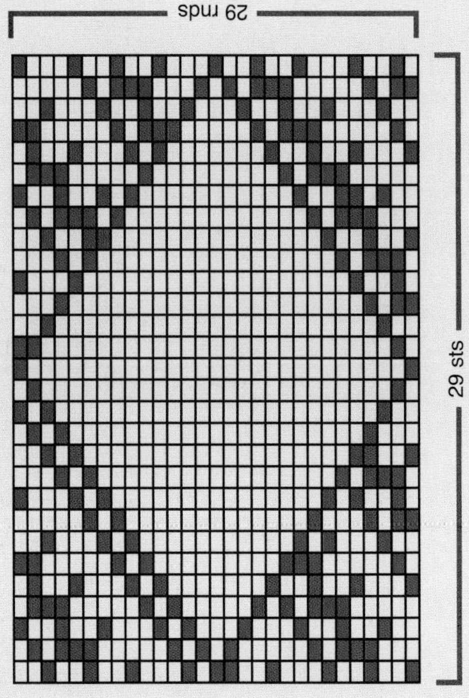
29 rnds
29 sts

Option D: Design Your Own

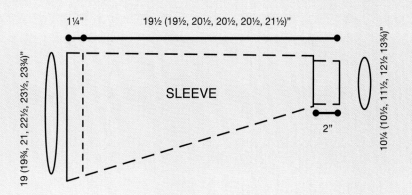

1¼" 19½ (19½, 20½, 20½, 20½, 21½)"

19 (19¾, 21, 22½, 23½, 23¾)"

10¼ (10½, 11½, 12½ 13¾)"

2"

SLEEVE

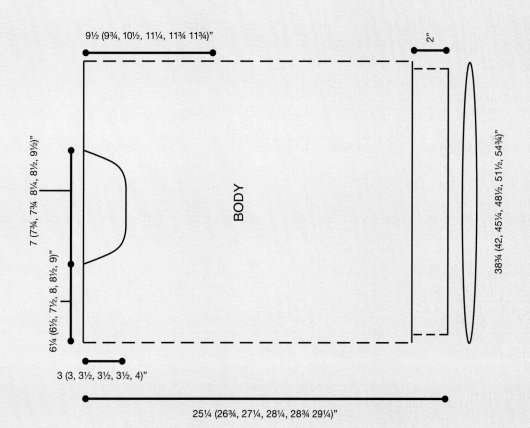

9½ (9¾, 10½, 11¼, 11¾ 11¾)"

2"

7 (7¾, 7¾ 8¼, 8½, 9½)"

6¼ (6½, 7½, 8, 8½, 9)"

38¾ (42, 45¼, 48½, 51½, 54¾)"

BODY

3 (3, 3½, 3½, 3½, 4)"

25¼ (26¾, 27¼, 28¼, 28¾ 29¼)"

Kids' Voss Sweaters

Sizes
Child's small (medium, large, X-large)
Instructions are given for smallest size, with larger sizes in parentheses. When only 1 number is given, it applies to all sizes.

Finished Measurements
Chest: 26 (27½, 30, 31½)"
Body Length: 17 (19, 21, 23)"
Sleeve Length to Underarm: 11 (13, 15, 16)"

Materials

- Cascade *220* (100% wool; 220 yds/100g per skein)
  Girl's version: 3 skeins Red #9404 (MC) and 1 skein each White #8505 (A) and Blue #7818 (B)
  Boy's version: 3 skeins Blue #7817 (MC) and 1 skein each White #8505 (A) and Red #9404 (B)
- Size 5 (3.75mm) double-pointed needles (set of 5), 16" and 24" circular needles
- Size 7 (4.5mm) double-pointed needles (set of 5) and 24" circular needles or size needed to obtain gauge
- Stitch markers, 1 in CC for beg of rnd
- Tapestry needle
- Cotton waste yarn for steeking
- Sewing machine

Gauge
20 sts and 24 rnds = 4" (10cm) in stranded 2-color St st with larger needles. *Adjust needle size as necessary to obtain correct gauge.*

These kids' sweaters are a simplified version of the heavily patterned adult sweater. This is a perfect set to make and wear as a family.

Pattern Stitch
Corrugated Ribbing (multiple of 4 sts)
Rnd 1: *K2 MC, p2 B; rep from * around.
Rep Rnd 1 for pat.

Special Technique
3-Needle Bind-Off: With RS tog and needles parallel, using a 3rd needle, knit tog a st from the front needle with 1 from the back. *Knit tog a st from the front and back needles, and slip the first st over the 2nd to bind off. Rep from * across, then fasten off last st.

Pattern Notes
- The body of the sweater is worked in the round from the bottom up. After knitting, the armhole positions are marked, reinforced by machine sewing, then cut. This is called "steeking" *(see sidebar, page 105).*
- The neck opening is also formed using a sew-and-cut method.
- The girl's version of the sweater includes a "lice pattern" on the body and sleeve of the sweater, as shown in the chart. Omit the lice pattern for the boy's version; work in solid color.
- When working sleeve, switch to 16" circular needle when there are enough stitches to do so.

Instructions

BODY

With smaller needle and B, CO 124 (132, 140, 148) sts; pm for beg of rnd and join, taking care not to twist sts.

Rnds 1–14: Join A and work in corrugated ribbing. Break B.

Inc rnd: Change to larger needle, join MC, and knit, increasing 6 (6, 10, 10) sts evenly around—130 (138, 150, 158) sts.

Preparation rnd: With MC, k65 (69, 75, 79), pm for side edge, k65 (69, 75, 79).

Work Kids' Chart; *beg where indicated for size being worked and working 32-st rep twice, then work to end point for size being worked, slip marker; rep from * for back.

Cont working charted pat as established through Rnd 27.

Girl's version only: Rep 12-rnd lice pat until piece measures approx 14 (16, 18, 20)", ending with 3 rnds MC.

Boy's version only: Work even in MC *only* until piece measures 14 (16, 18, 20)".

Both versions: Work 15-rnd Shoulder pat, completing chart.

Place sts (including side st markers) on waste yarn to hold for sewing armholes and neck opening.

SLEEVE

With smaller dpns and B, CO 36 (36, 40, 40) sts; pm for beg of rnd and join, taking care not to twist sts.

Join A and work 2" in corrugated ribbing. Break B.

Inc rnd: Change to larger needle, join MC, and knit, increasing 4 (4, 6, 6) sts evenly around—40 (40, 46, 46) sts.

Next rnd: Knit with MC.

Work 15-rnd Shoulder pat, then work 12-rnd lice pat (Girl's version) or solid MC (Boy's version); *at the same time,* work Inc rnd [every 3 rnds] 6 (12, 0, 2) times, then [every 4 rnds] 9 (6, 18, 18) times, working new sts into established pat, as follows:

Inc rnd: K1, M1, knit to end of rnd, M1—70 (76, 82, 86) sts when inc rnds are complete.

Work even until sleeve measures 11 (13, 15, 16)" or desired length.

FACING

Beg working back and forth in rev St st with MC. *(See alphabet chart sidebar on page 114 for directions on placing a secret message in the facing)*

Row 1 (RS): Purl.

Row 2: K1, M1, knit to last st, M1, k1—72 (78, 84, 88) sts.

Row 3: P1, M1, purl to last st, M1, p1—74 (80, 86, 90) sts.

Rep Rows 2 and 3 twice more—82 (88, 94, 98) sts.

Place sts on waste yarn for holder.

Finishing

Weave in ends. Block to finished measurements.

Close up of girl's Voss pattern

CUT ARMHOLES

Mark armhole depth below markers indicating sides of body. Using a contrasting piece of cotton yarn, baste a line from side marker to marked armhole depth position, going between 2 side edge sts. *(See sidebar on page 107.)* After sewing in sleeves, loosely sew live sts of facing to WS of armhole, covering cut edge.

NECKLINE MARK AND SEW

On front of sweater, mark off 19 (20, 22, 24) sts on each side of neck for shoulders. Slip rem 27 (29, 31, 31) sts to separate holder for neck. Mark neck depth 3" down from center front neck. Using a piece of cotton yarn, baste the shape of neckline around front of sweater. With machine, sew along the marked neck 2 times. Cut out crescent, leaving ¾" seam allowance from sewn line.

SHOULDER JOIN

Join shoulder seams using 3-needle BO.

NECK EDGING

With smaller 16" circular needle, pick up and knit 76 (76, 80, 80) sts around neck as follows: *2A, 2B, rep from * around.
Work 6 rnds in corrugated rib. Break A.

FACING

Rnd 1: With B, knit.
Rnd 2: Purl.
Rnds 3–8: *K2, p2; rep from * around.
Fold facing inside neck line and secure by loosely sewing live sts to pickup rnd on the inside.

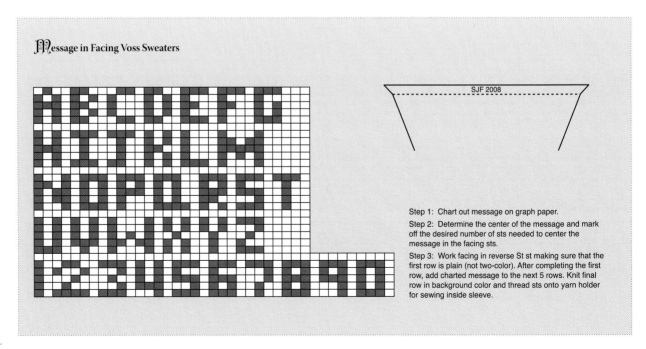

Message in Facing Voss Sweaters

SJF 2008

Step 1: Chart out message on graph paper.

Step 2: Determine the center of the message and mark off the desired number of sts needed to center the message in the facing sts.

Step 3: Work facing in reverse St st making sure that the first row is plain (not two-color). After completing the first row, add charted message to the next 5 rows. Knit final row in background color and thread sts onto yarn holder for sewing inside sleeve.

KID'S VOSS CHART

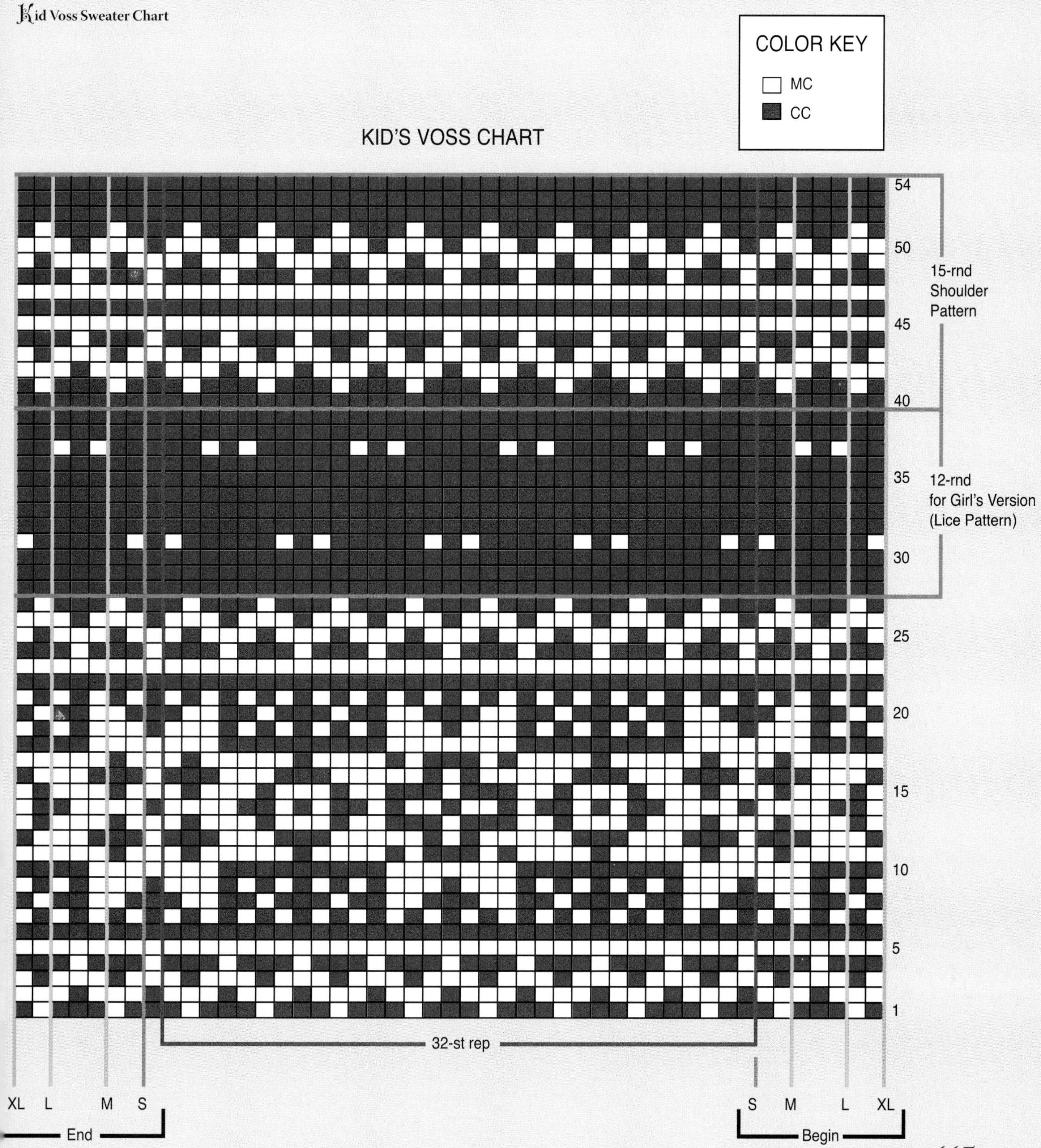

COLOR KEY
☐ MC
■ CC

15-rnd
Shoulder
Pattern

12-rnd
for Girl's Version
(Lice Pattern)

54
50
45
40
35
30
25
20
15
10
5
1

32-st rep

XL L M S

End

S M L XL

Begin

115

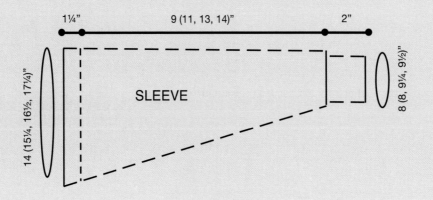

1¼"   9 (11, 13, 14)"   2"

14 (15¼, 16½, 17¼)"

SLEEVE

8 (8, 9¼, 9½)"

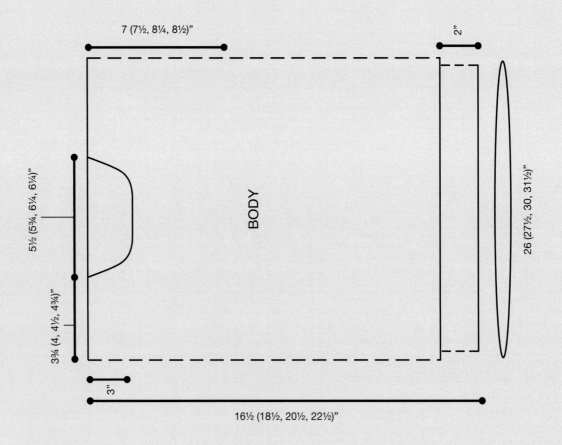

7 (7½, 8¼, 8½)"   2"

5½ (5¾, 6¼, 6¼)"

3¾ (4, 4½, 4¾)"

BODY

26 (27½, 30, 31½)"

3"

16½ (18½, 20½, 22½)"

Voss Self-Fringing Shawl

In addition to providing inspiration for the Voss Family Sweaters, the cross-stitch motifs in the embroidered headscarf were used to create the Voss Self-Fringing Shawl.

The design along the edge of the shawl uses six different diamond patterns drawn from the original piece. The inner pattern on the shawl is called the Tree of Life and appears to grow from the center out. It is interesting to note that this main pattern consists of a simple two-row repeat that is shifted over every other row to create the branchlike appearance of the "tree."

Finished Measurements
Width along top of shawl: 66"
Length down center of shawl: 32"

Materials

- Blackberry Ridge *Mer-Made DK Wool* (100% superwash merino wool; 260 yds/114g [4 oz.] skein) 3 skeins Black (MC) and 2 skeins Natural Cream (CC)
- Size 5 (3.75mm) 30" circular needle
- Size 7 (4.5mm) 30" circular needle or size needed to obtain gauge
- Tapestry needle

Gauge
24 sts and 27 rows = 4" (10cm) in stranded 2-color St st with larger needle.
Adjust needle size as necessary to obtain correct gauge.

Pattern Notes
- The shawl is self-fringing and is worked with the right side facing you on every row. Attach and break the yarn at the beginning and end of each row, leaving 6" tails at both ends. After completing two rows, tie the four yarn tails together with an overhand knot to make fringe at both edges of the shawl.
- The charted pattern shows only the right half of the shawl. The other half of the shawl is worked as a mirror image of the charted pattern. The center stitch of the shawl, shown on the chart at the left edge and bordered in red, should *not* be repeated when repeating the pattern for the left half of the shawl.

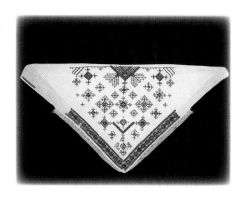

This skaut or headscarf, which inspired the motifs that appear along the border of the Voss Shawl, was probably made and worn by Ingeborg Larsdatter Lillethun of Vossestrand, Norway. Ingeborg immigrated in 1891 to Boone County, Illinois. She died in 1909.

Instructions

With larger needle and MC, leaving a 6" tail, CO 3 sts; break yarn, leaving a 6" tail.

Start from right edge of knitting and work chart.

Row 1: Attach MC, leaving a 6" tail; k1f&b, k1, k1f&b; break yarn, leaving a 6" tail—5 sts.

Row 2: Attach both MC and CC, leaving a 6" tail; k1f&b, k3 following chart, k1f&b; break both yarns, leaving 6" tails.

Continue working chart, increasing in the first and last st of each row, attaching new yarns at beg of each row and breaking them at end, leaving 6" tails, and tying 4 yarn tails together at each edge after completing 2 rows.

Complete 101-row chart once, then rep from A to B.

FACING

Change to smaller needle; work back and forth.

Rows 1 (RS) and 2: Knit with MC.

Row 3: K1, ssk, knit to last 3 sts, k2tog, k1.

Row 4: P1, p2tog, purl to last 3 sts, ssp, p1.

Rep [Rows 3 and 4] twice more.

BO very loosely with larger needle in right hand.

Block shawl and facing.

Fold facing and sew to WS; keep sts loose (do not pull too tight) to maintain the elasticity of the fabric.

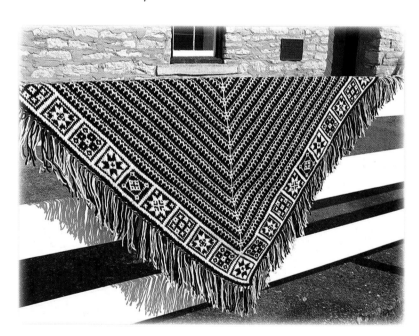

Voss Shawl Chart

KEY

■	MC
□	CC
▭	Center Stitch
│	A/B--Rep between these lines

B
100
95
90
85
80
75
70
65
60
55
50
45
40
35
30
25
20
A
15
10
5
CO
Center Stitch

4

Adventurous Techniques

Never be afraid to step out into new territory. Imagine the sense of adventure that each immigrant must have had to make the big migration to America. This chapter offers some interesting projects that will challenge and satisfy the need for something different. The adventure of entrelac knitting can be explored by making the Entrelac Wristers or the Entrelac Sheep. The Viking Pillow offers a challenge in the applied twisted I-cord trim that is knit as it is attached to the finished pillow. The Foolish Virgin Pillow challenges the knitter with multiple colors carried along the back of the work, utilizes the steek, and finishes off with the twisted I-cord trim.

Entrelac Wristers

Finished Measurements
Circumference: 7"
Width: 5 ½"

Materials

- Dale of Norway *Heilo* (100% wool; 109 yds/50g per ball): 1 ball each Tartan Green #7562 (A), Moss Green #9335 (B), Sand Heather #0004 (C), and Grey Heather #0007 (D)
- Size 4 (3.5mm) double-pointed needles (set of 5) or 11" circular needles or size needed to obtain gauge

Gauge
24 sts and 30 rows = 4" (10cm) in St st.
Adjust needle size as necessary to obtain correct gauge.

The only piece of entrelac knitting at Vesterheim is a pair of knee-length red and black entrelac socks. The socks, which belonged to Jensine Nelson Hansen of Vefsen, Norway, were brought to Wisconsin in 1889 and donated to the museum in 1971. Because they use a technique rarely seen in Norwegian knitting, the socks are featured in the knitting display in the museum.

The entrelac or "basket-weave" technique is most commonly recognized as a Finnish knitting technique. Entrelac is fun to learn. Although it appears as if the squares are sewn together, the squares are actually joined to each other as they are knit. With each completed square comes a feeling of satisfaction and the anticipation of moving on to the next square.

Special Abbreviations
(See Knitting from Left to Right sidebar, page 124)
KLR: Knit from left to right
WB: Work back

Pattern Stitch
Garter Chevron (multiple of 12 sts)
Rnd 1: *K1, yo, k4, S2KP2, k4, yo; rep from * around.
Rnd 2: Purl.
Rep Rnds 1 and 2 for pat.

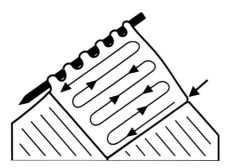

Figure 1

Figure 2

These socks belonged to Jensine Nelson Hansen (b. 1872) of Vefsen, Norway, and were brought to Wisconsin in 1889.

Pattern Notes

- The wrister begins with a garter stitch chevron pattern that fits into the square entrelac pattern.
- If using double-pointed needles, you may need to shift the stitches from one needle to another during the entrelac section.

Instructions

STEP 1: GARTER CHEVRON

Using long-tail method and A, CO 48 sts; pm for beg of rnd and join, taking care not to twist sts.

Purl 1 rnd.

Work Garter Chevron pat in following stripe sequence: 2 rnds each B, C, D, A, B, C.

STEP 2: FIRST SET OF SQUARES (Left-Leaning)

With D, mark into sets of 12 sts and work four squares.

First Square (Left-Leaning) *See Figure 1.*

Row 1: K6.

Row 2: (WB) Sl 1, KLR5.

Row 3: Sl 1, k4, k2tog-tbl (1 st in D and 1 in C).

Rep [Rows 2 and 3] 5 more times. Square complete.

Rep around to make 4 left-leaning squares with D.

First round of squares complete. Break D.

STEP 3: SECOND SET OF SQUARES (Right-Leaning)

With C, work 4 right-leaning squares.

With RH needle, pick up 6 loops (without knitting them) along slip-st edge of first square, then attach C at tip of square and begin knitting backward.

Row 1: (WB) KLR6, turn. *See Figure 2.*

Row 2: Sl 1, k5, turn.

Row 3: (WB) Sl 1, KLR4, KLR2tog, turn. *NOTE: This joins the newly forming square to the sts of the last square worked on previous round.*

Rep [Rows 2 and 3] 5 more times. Square complete.

Rep around to make 4 right-leaning squares with C. 2nd round of squares complete. Break C.

STEP 4: THIRD SET OF SQUARES (Left-Leaning)

With LH needle, pick up 6 loops (without knitting them) along slip-st edge of first square, then attach D at tip of square and begin knitting forward.

Complete square following Step 2.

Rep for rem 3 squares. Break D.

STEP 5: GARTER CHEVRON

Rnd 1: With C, working from right to left, *k6 live sts of next square, pick up and knit 6 sts along slip-st edge; rep from * around, pm for beg of rnd—48 sts.

Rnd 2: Purl.

Work Garter Chevron pat in following stripe sequence: 2 rnds each B, A, D, C, B, C. On last (purl) rnd of C, bind off very loosely pwise.

Finishing
Weave in ends. Block.

Knitting from Left to Right

Before beginning the adventure of entrelac, it is helpful to learn how to knit from left to right (KLR). KLR is worked when you would normally turn the work and purl back. With the use of this technique, you can knit "backward" without turning the work; this eliminates the need to turn the fabric back and forth on 6 stitches. Many knitters have found this technique helpful when making bobbles or working the heel of a sock. Learning how to KLR will make entrelac knitting much more enjoyable.

Special Abbreviations
KLR: Knit from left to right
WB: Work back

To knit a practice swatch in stockinette stitch using this technique:
Cast on 20 sts.
Row 1: Knit.
Row 2 (WB): *Without turning*, work back (WB) using the KLR technique.
Row 3: *Without turning*, knit.
It may seem awkward at first, but a few minutes of trying this out will make the entrelac knitting experience more rewarding and less frustrating.

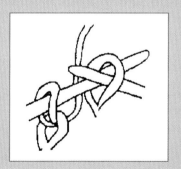

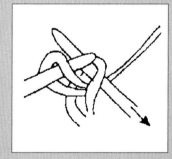

Step 1:

With LH needle, go through the *back* of the first st on RH needle.

Step 2:

Wrap yarn *over* the LH needle counterclockwise.

Step 3:

Draw newly formed st through old sts and slide RH needle out of old st, leaving new st on LH needle.

Dream Weaver

Weaver Syvilla Tweed Bolson is known for throwing herself into her work. Literally. The last time we saw her in Decorah, Iowa, she was working with a student to warp one of the looms at Vesterheim and was actually standing *in* the loom, becoming one with the frame and fiber. As she weaves traditional Norwegian-style cloth in her Decorah home, Syvilla creates a tangible connection between past Norwegian woven traditions and the present. Syvilla has won awards for the excellence of her work, and she celebrates these accomplishments by teaching others to weave so that the traditions may continue on.

With a maiden name of "Tweed," Syvilla was practically born into the world of textiles. A visit to Syvilla's home always involves a much-anticipated tour of what's on the looms, talk about the latest classes she is teaching, and, the best part, a lot of show and tell.

Evidence of her lifelong interest in Norwegian weaving and textiles exists throughout the home she and her husband, Marlin, built and have

shared with their family for the past fifty-eight years. On her porch stand looms with her works in progress, her walls are covered with her woven masterpieces, and the pillows on her couch showcase samplers of her work. But it's her basement that is the real wonder. Syvilla's basement is home to her floor looms and to her traditional Norwegian weaving, knitting yarn, pattern, and supply import business. Her business got its start when students began to ask her where she got her fibers. They inquired so often that she decided to open a shop that she unofficially calls Tweeds and Fleeces.

With every movement of her shuttle, Syvilla is sharing her passion by teaching others from all over the world about traditional Norwegian weaving techniques. Syvilla has an unsinkable spirit and is not afraid to learn from whoever will teach her, including the many people who come to her for instruction and inspiration. We are not weavers, yet we do see the knitting possibilities inherent in the traditional warp and weft threads of Syvilla's works.

Entrelac Sheep

The Entrelac Sheep are knit following the same set of directions used for the Entrelac Wristers. Different-size sheep are achieved by using progressively thicker yarn and larger needles. Each sheep contains fifty-four squares, thirteen triangles, four legs, two ears, and one tail—oh my!

Special Technique

Provisional Cast-On: With crochet hook and waste yarn, make a chain several sts longer than desired cast-on. With knitting needle and project yarn, pick up indicated number of sts in the "bumps" on back of chain. When indicated in pattern, "unzip" the crochet chain to free live sts.

Sizes
Small (Medium, Large)
Instructions are the same for all sizes; each size is achieved by using different yarn and needles.

Finished Measurements
Height: 9 (12, 17)"
Length: 12 (15, 20)"

Materials

- Small: Reynolds *Lite Lopi* (100% Icelandic wool; 109yds/50g per ball): 1 ball each Black #0059 (MC) and Red #0414 (CC)

- Medium: Reynolds *Original Lopi* (100% Icelandic wool; 110yds/100g per ball): 2 balls Green #0737 (MC) and 1 ball Rust #9971(CC)

- Large: Reynolds *Bulky Lopi* (100% Icelandic wool; 67 yds/100g per ball): 2 balls each Natural Tan #0085 (MC) and Natural White #0601(CC)
- Size 6 (9, 11) [3.5 (5.5, 8)mm] double-pointed needles (set of 5) and 16" (24", 36") circular needles or size needed to obtain gauge
- Crochet hook same size as needles used
- 2 safety pins
- Stitch markers
- Tapestry needle
- Fiberfill stuffing

Gauge
18 (14, 10) sts and 28 (24, 14) rows = 4" (10cm) in St st.
Adjust needle size as necessary to obtain correct gauge.

Detail of Jansine Nelson Hansen's entrelac socks.

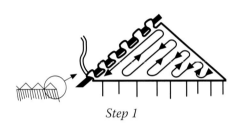

Step 1

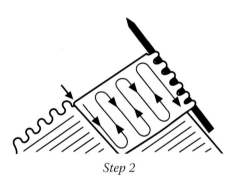

Step 2

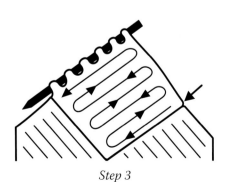

Step 3

Pattern Notes

- All 3 Entrelac Sheep are knit following the same set of directions. The different sizes are achieved by using progressively thicker yarn and larger needles. Each sheep contains fifty-four entrelac squares, thirteen triangles, four legs, two ears, and one tail.
- The belly of the sheep is worked first as a square, then stitches are picked up around the belly square to work entrelac, which forms the sheep's body and head.
- Legs, ears, and tail are worked separately and sewn on.
- The method of working the pickup row for each entrelac square is a refinement of the method used for the "beginner" wristers.

Instructions

BELLY

Using provisional method and MC, CO 32 sts.
Row 1: Purl.
Row 2: *Sl 1, k1; rep from * to end.
Row 3: Sl 1, purl to end.
Rep [Rows 2 and 3] 7 times. Do not cut yarn.

Use dpns as needed to pick up around belly square.
Pickup rnd: With working yarn, pick up and knit 8 sts along slip-st edge; unzip provisional CO, place 32 live sts onto spare needle and knit across; pick up and knit 8 sts along the other slip-st edge, pm for beg of rnd—80 sts total around belly square.
Setup rnd: *[K2, k2tog] twice, pm; rep from * around—60 sts.
There should be 4 sets of 6 marked-off sts along each side of the belly and 1 set of 6 marked-off sts on each end. With safety pins, mark one end as the rump and the other as the head end of the sheep.

ENTRELAC DIRECTIONS

Step 1: Base Triangles
In this first step, triangles are worked back and forth using MC.
Row 1 (RS): Sl 1, k2. *See Figure 1.*
Row 2 (WB): S1, KLR2.
Row 3: Sl 1, k3.
Row 4 (WB): Sl 1, KLR3.
Row 5: Sl 1, k4.
Row 6 (WB): Sl 1, KLR4.
Row 7: Sl 1, k5. End of triangle. Mark first triangle with a safety pin or other marker.
Rep Rows 1–7 until there are 10 triangles around the belly of the sheep.

Step 2: First Set of Squares (Right-Leaning)
With RH needle pick up 5 loops along the slip-st edge of the first triangle (the first one worked). *NOTE: Pick up loops from the slip-st edge without knitting into loops.* Attach CC at the tip of the first triangle and begin knitting left to right for row.

Row 1 (WB): KLR the 5 loops that were picked up and KLR 1 st from the set of CC sts of the 10th triangle to make a total of 6 sts to work for the square. *See Figure 2.*

Row 2: Sl 1, k5.

Row 3 (WB): Sl 1, KLR4, KLR2tog (1 st in CC and 1 st in MC). *NOTE: This joins the newly forming square to the sts from the previously formed triangle.*

Rep [Rows 2 and 3] 4 times. Square complete. Mark first square with safety pin.

With RH needle, pick up 5 loops along the slip-st edge of the next triangle.

Rep around to make 10 CC squares.

Step 3: Second Set of Squares (Left-Leaning)

With LH needle, pick up 5 loops along slip-st edge of first square, then attach MC at tip of square and begin knitting forward.

Row 1 (RS): K5 in loops that were picked up, k1 from the 6 sts of the 10th square. *See Figure 3.*

Row 2 (WB): Sl 1, KLR5.

Row 3: Sl 1, k4, k2tog-tbl (1 st in MC and 1 in CC)

Rep [Rows 2 and 3] 4 more times. Square complete.

Pick up 5 more loops along the slip-st edge of the next square.

Rep around to make 10 MC squares.

Step 4: Third Set of Squares

With CC, pick up loops along first left-leaning square. Rep Step 2.

Step 5: Fourth Set of Squares

With MC, rep Step 3. The last square formed will be the center back or "rump" square; mark this square.

SEW RUMP

To form the rump shape, sew the MC square that is above the marked "rump" position to the edges of the MC square on either side of the "rump." (In other words: Attach the slip-st edge from the 10th square (rump) to the "live" sts on the 9th square and join the "live" sts from the 10th square (rump) to the slip-st edge of the first square.) *See Sew rump.*

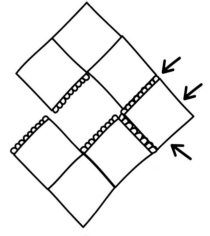

Sew rump

Step 6: Fifth Set of Squares

With CC, work 6 squares as in Step 2. Start at the 9th square slip-st edge and pick up loops along edge. Stop after completing the 6th square.

SEW BACK

Break yarn leaving a 12″ tail and sew the 2 back CC squares to the MC squares along the 4 edges to close center back seam.

Step 7: Sixth Set of Squares—Neck

Mark center front. Starting at center front, attach MC a first st left of center front. *See Sew back.*

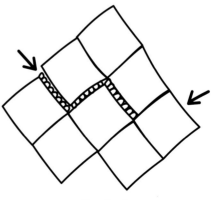

Sew back

First Triangle for Left Edge of Face
Row 1: K1f&b.
Row 2 (WB): Sl 1, KLR1.
Row 3: K1f&b, ssk.
Row 4 (WB): Sl 1, KLR2.
Row 5: K1f&b, k1, ssk.
Row 6 (WB): Sl 1, KLR3.
Row 7: K1f&b, k2, ssk.
Row 8 (WB): Sl 1, KLR4.
Row 9: K1f&b, k3, ssk.
Row 10 (WB): Sl 1, KLR5.
Row 11: K1f&b, k4, ssk.
With MC, work 3 squares as in Step 3 for the left side, back, and right side of head.

Second Triangle for Right Edge of Face
Pick up 6 loops along slip-st edge of the next CC square.
Row 1: K6.
Row 2 (WB): KLR2tog, KLR4.
Row 3: Sl 1, k4.
Row 4 (WB): KLR2tog, KLR3.
Row 5: Sl 1, k3.
Row 6 (WB): KLR2tog, KLR2.
Row 7: Sl 1, k2.
Row 8 (WB): KLR2tog, KLR1.
Row 9: Sl 1, k1.
Row 10 (WB): KLR2tog.

Step 8: Seventh Set of Squares
Pick up 5 loops along slip-st edge of last triangle formed, attach CC at the tip of the triangle and work as in Step 2, making 4 squares. Join top back of head by sewing the sts of the 2nd square to the slip-st edge of the 3rd square.

Step 9: Top of Head Triangle
With MC, rep instructions for first triangle for top of head.
With MC, make one last square following Step 3. Join top of head by attaching the MC squares to the CC squares of the previous step.

FACE
The face opening is the stuffing point for the sheep. Stuff to desired firmness. Add more stuffing once the face is completed, before closing final portion.
Starting at chin, pick up and knit 30 sts around opening; pm for beg of rnd.
Rnd 1 and all odd rnds: Knit.
Rnd 2: *K1, ssk, k9, k2tog, k1; rep from * once—26 sts.
Rnd 4: *K1, ssk, k7, k2tog, k1; rep from * once—22 sts.
Rnd 6: *K1, ssk, k5, k2tog, k1; rep from * once—18 sts.

Rnd 8: *K1, ssk, k3, k2tog, k1; rep from * once—14 sts.
Rnd 10: *K1, ssk, k1, k2tog, k1; rep from * once—10 sts.
Break yarn leaving an 8" tail. With tapestry needle, thread tail through rem sts, but do not close. Stuff face portion, pull tight, and secure end.

LEGS (make 4)
With dpns and MC, CO 24 sts; pm for beg of rnd and join, taking care not to twist sts. Attach CC.
Rnds 1–5: *K1 MC, p1 CC; rep from * around. Break CC.
Rnd 6: Knit.
Rnds 7–18: Purl.
Rnd 19: *P1, p2tog; rep from * around—18 sts.
Rnd 20: Purl.
Rnd 21: P2tog around—9 sts.
Break yarn leaving a 6" tail.

With tapestry needle, thread tail through rem sts, pull tight, and secure.

Fold at purl edge so that St st side of leg is on outside and ribbed cuff is folded back. Stuff and sew to corner of belly square, attaching along purl ridge of leg where cuff is folded back.

Make 3 more legs and sew to other 3 corners of belly square.

TAIL
With dpns and MC, CO 9 sts; pm for beg of rnd and join, taking care not to twist sts.
Knit 8 rnds.
Break yarn, leaving a 6" tail.
With tapestry needle, thread tail through sts, pull tight, and secure end.
Sew cast-on edge of tail onto rump square.

EARS (make 2)
CO 12 sts.
Rows 1–10: K9, yf, sl 3.
Work I-cord BO as follows: *K2, ssk, pass 3 sts back to RH needle; rep from * to last 3 sts. Put first and last 3 sts on separate dpns and join with Kitchener st.
Attach CO edge to top of head.

Gardsjord farm, Rauland, Telemark, Norway, 1890s.

GAUSTA COLLECTION, VESTERHEIM ARCHIVE

Viking Pillow

Artifacts provided by Sam the Viking

Finished Measurements
14" x 14"

Materials:

- Cascade *220* (100% wool; 220yds/100g skein): 2 skeins each Blue #7818 (MC) and White #8505 (CC); 1 skein Red #9404 (A)
- Size 7 (4.5mm) 24" double-pointed needles (set of 2) and circular needles or size needed to obtain gauge
- Medium-size crochet hook
- Stitch markers, 1 in CC for beg of rnd
- 14" square pillow form
- Tapestry needle

Gauge
20 sts and 26 rnds = 4" (10cm) in stranded 2-color St st.
Adjust needle size as necessary to obtain correct gauge.

The focal point of the Viking Pillow was drawn from a tapestry weaving that depicts three ships on the ocean framed by a border of birds and maidens (see page 131). The artifacts shown with the pillow in this photo are used courtesy of Sam the Viking.

Special Techniques
Provisional Cast-On: With crochet hook and waste yarn, make a chain several sts longer than desired cast-on. With knitting needle and project yarn, pick up indicated number of sts in the "bumps" on back of chain. When indicated in pattern, "unzip" the crochet chain to free live sts.

Applied Twisted I-Cord Edging: See sidebar on page 132.

Pattern Notes
- The pillow is worked in the round.
- The chart is knit with MC and CC only; the small red sections are duplicate-stitched after pillow is complete.
- I-cord edging is applied after the pillow has been stuffed and sewn together. Directions are given for the applied twisted I-cord, which is attached as it is knit. If you must, the I-cord can be knit separately and then sewn on, but the applied technique is preferred.

Reconstructed Viking ship at the World's Columbian Exposition, Chicago, Illinois, 1893.
PHOTO BY COPELIN, CHICAGO, ILLINOIS. VESTERHEIM ARCHIVE

Instructions

Using provisional method and MC, CO 136 sts; place marker and join, taking care not to twist sts.

Follow chart, repeating the Viking ship motif twice around the pillow and working "red" stitches in white (CC).

Continue until 77-rnd chart is complete.

Slip sts of 2nd rep of chart to a separate needle and graft top front and back sts of pillow tog using Kitchener st.

With tapestry needle and A, work the red stitches using duplicate st.

Finishing

Weave in ends and block pillow.

Stuff with pillow form.

Unzip provisional cast-on, slipping front and back sts to separate needles; graft bottom front and back sts tog using Kitchener st.

Follow Applied Twisted I-Cord instructions to complete edging.

The sailor's toast is presented by the captain of the ship on the night before reaching port. This quote is from Henrik Ibsen's play *Kjaerlighetens Komedie*:

*"Og har jeg enn seilet min
skute paa grunn,
O, saa var det dog deilig
aa fare!"*

Translation:
"And even if I had sailed
my ship up on the shoals,
Oh, but it was still a hell
of a nice trip!"

The tapestry that inspired the Viking Pillow was designed by the Norwegian painter Frederik Collet and woven by Aagot Lund from Ørje, Norway. It was purchased by the donor in Oslo in 1936. LUTHER COLLEGE COLLECTION

Applied Twisted I-cord

This I-cord is attached to the edges of the pillow as it is knit; there's no need to sew it on afterward. Two separate I-cords are worked simultaneously, each twisted around the other, then attached to the main pillow fabric. Five-inch double-pointed needles are the perfect tools for working this technique. One I-cord is worked with MC, the other with CC.

Unattached I-cord: With dpns, CO 3 sts. K3, *do not turn work, place RH needle in left hand and slip sts to other end of dpn, wrap yarn around back of work and k3 **Rnd 1:** *K3, do not turn work, place RH needle in left hand and slip sts to other end of dpn, wrap yarn around back of work, ready to knit; rep from * until cord is desired length; rep Rnd 1 as indicated in pattern.

Mark every 3rd st around all 4 edges of the pillow. Starting at lower corner, *work 3 rnds of unattached I-cord with MC, and after last rnd, pick up (but do not knit) 1 marked st from pillow edge and place on left end of LH needle.

Next rnd: K2, k2tog-tbl (attaching MC I-cord to pillow edge). Work 8 rnds of unattached I-cord with MC. Start 2nd I-cord with CC. Work 3 rnds of unattached I-cord, then pick up the next marked st from the pillow edge and place on left end of LH needle.

Next rnd: K2, k2tog-tbl (attaching CC I-cord to pillow edge). Work 8 rnds of unattached I-cord with CC. Twist MC around CC and repeat from * around pillow.

Attaching and twisting I-cords.

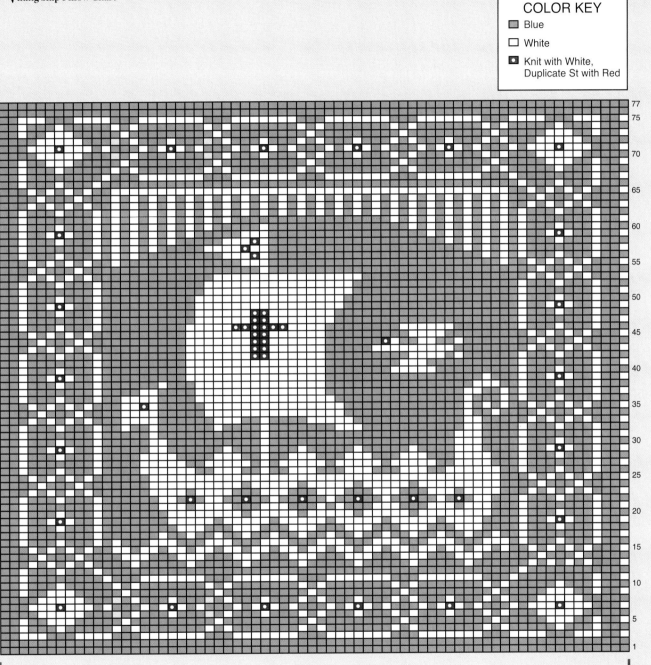

COLOR KEY
- Blue
- White
- Knit with White, Duplicate St with Red

68-st rep

77
75
70
65
60
55
50
45
40
35
30
25
20
15
10
5
1

Foolish Virgins Pillow

Finished Measurements
29" x 18" (blocked)

Materials

- Cascade *220* (100% wool; 220 yds/100g per skein): 1 skein each Cream #8010 (A), Straw #8412 (B), Salmon Heather #2451 (C), Shell Pink #7804 (D), Sage #8234 (E), Forest #9429 (F), and Brick Red #2413 (G)
- Size 7 (4.5mm) 24" circular needle or size needed to obtain gauge
- Approx 1 ¼ yds tightly woven muslin for pillow form
- 1 yd total of coordinating fabric for pillow back *(see Pattern Notes)*
- Thread in coordinating color
- Fiberfill or other stuffing material
- Sewing needle
- Sewing machine
- Tapestry needle

Gauge
23 sts and 18 rnds = 4" (10cm) in stranded St st.
Adjust needle size as necessary to obtain correct gauge.

We discovered this pattern on a stylized tunic in the museum collection. The maker may have been inspired by the Norwegian folk story that in turn was inspired by a Bible verse. To read about the wise and foolish virgins, check out Matthew 25:1–13, the parable of the ten virgins.

This pillow incorporates many of the techniques used to create a Norwegian sweater and a few other talents. You will carry colors, most often more than two in a row; prepare and cut a steek; make a twisted cord; and use your sewing skills. Don't let its size fool you—you'd be wise to try it!

Pattern Notes
- This pillow front is worked in the round with a steek, then cut open for a flat piece. The steek is made by purling the first 3 stitches of every round.
- The pillow back is fabric; the sample uses 9 different fabrics pieced together.
- Since this pillow size is unique, you will make your own pillow form.

Instructions
With G, CO 174 sts, pm for beg of rnd and join, taking care not to twist sts.

Setup rnd: P3 (for steek), work chart in St st over next 171 sts (5 pat reps + last st of chart)

Purling first 3 sts of every rnd, complete chart.

With G, BO.

Block lightly.

Secure the steek with machine stitching, then cut. *(See page 107 for steek instructions.)*

Block the piece again.

Assembly

PILLOW FORM

Measure the dimensions of pillow front after cutting steek. Add 2" to height and width measurements so that the finished pillow form is slightly larger than the knitted pillow front. It's good to have a bit of tension on the knitted fabric to keep the pillow front taut, preventing it from stretching out.

Cut 2 pieces of muslin to the measurements determined above.

With right sides of muslin tog and using ¼" seam allowance, machine-sew pieces together, leaving center third of one short side open.

Turn right side out. Stuff, making sure that the stuffing is firm, but still soft enough to be squeezable. The corners are trickiest to stuff—start with them, then fill in the middle. After stuffing, hand-sew the opening closed.

PILLOW BACK

Add 2 ½" to height and width measurements of pillow front and cut fabric to those dimensions. If desired, sew multiple pieces of coordinating fabric together to make 1 large piece, then cut to appropriate dimensions.

With right sides of knitted front and fabric back facing each other, baste pieces together, working at edges of knitted front and leaving a ¼" seam allowance on back; stretch knitted piece as necessary to match fabric; leave center third of one short side open. Machine-sew over the basting lines.

Turn the piece right side out. Being careful not to rip the stitching, insert the pillow form through the open edge. Hand-sew the opening.

Make twisted cord following instructions on page 136.

With tapestry needle and one of the yarn colors in the twisted cord, sew cord to edge of pillow at sewing seam.

This woman's embroidered shirt is from East Telemark, Norway, eighteenth century. LUTHER COLLEGE COLLECTION

Matthew 25:1–13

"And five of them were wise, and five were foolish. They that were foolish took their lamps, and took no oil with them. But the wise took oil in their vessels with their lamps. While the bridegroom tarried, they all slumbered and slept. And at midnight there was a cry made, Behold, the bridegroom cometh; go ye out to meet him. Then all those virgins arose, and trimmed their lamps. And the foolish said unto the wise, Give us of your oil; for our lamps are gone out. But the wise answered, saying, Not so; lest there be not enough for us and you: but go ye rather to them that sell, and buy for yourselves. And while they went to buy, the bridegroom came; and they that were ready went in with him to the marriage: and the door was shut. Afterward came also the other virgins, saying, Lord, Lord, open to us. But he answered and said, Verily I say unto you, I know you not. Watch therefore, for ye know neither the day nor the hour wherein the Son of man cometh."

Twisted Cord Directions

Figure 1

Figure 2

Figure 3

Figure 4

Figure 5

Figure 6

Step 1: Measure around all 4 sides of the finished pillow.

Step 2: Multiply total circumference by 5 to get the length to cut your yarn for the cord. Cut the number of strands you will use and knot them together. *Note: These will be very long strands of yarn, but the length will shorten considerably as the strands are twisted; it's also better to have too much and cut the finished cord than have too little and not have enough cord to fit around the edge of the pillow.*

Step 3: Work as a team of two or find a stationary object to which to anchor one end of the knotted yarn—a doorknob is good. *(See Figure 1.)* If working in a pair, each person should hold one end of the knotted yarn, stand far enough apart that the yarn is taut but not tight, then twist counterclockwise. If the yarn is tied to a stationary object, stand back from the door so that the yarn is taut but not tight, and twist counterclockwise. *(See Figure 2.)*

Step 4: Continue twisting until the yarn twists back on itself when you give it some slack. *(See Figure 3.)*

Step 5: Fold twisted cord in half. This can be tricky, and it is especially helpful to have another set of hands so the cord doesn't become a twisted mess. *(See Figure 4.)*

Step 6: Hold on to the original two ends opposite the fold in the cord. Then let go of the rest of the cord and let it twist on itself. *(See Figure 5.)*

Step 7: Straighten out and untangle any knots. *(See Figure 6.)*

Step 8: Tie a knot in the end opposite the fold. You will tie it like the end of a balloon—an overhand knot. *(See Figure 7 and Figure 8.)*

Step 9: Finished knot. *(See Figure 9.)*

Figure 7

Figure 8

Figure 9

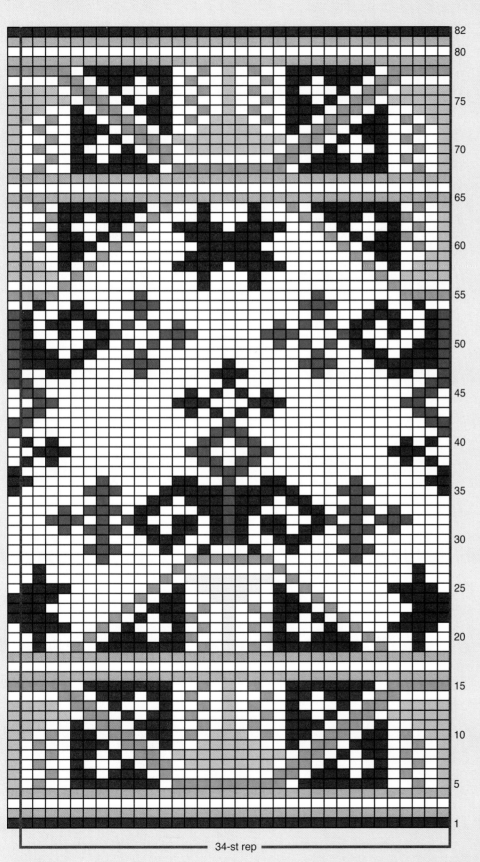

82
80

75

70

65

60

55

50

45

40

35

30

25

20

15

10

5

1

34-st rep

COLOR KEY

- ☐ Cream (A)
- ☐ Straw (B)
- ▨ Salmon Heather (C)
- ▨ Shell Pink (D)
- ▨ Sage (E)
- ■ Forest (F)
- ■ Brick Red (G)

Abbreviations

beg . . . . begin, beginning, begins

BO . . . . bind off

CC . . . . contrast color

cm . . . . centimeter(s)

CO . . . . cast on

cont . . . . continue, continuing

dec(s) . . . . decrease, decreasing, decreases

dpn . . . . double-pointed needle(s)

est . . . . establish, established

foll . . . . follow(s), following

inc(s) . . . . increase(s), increasing

k . . . . knit

k1f&b . . . . knit into front then back of same st (increase)

k1f,b,&f . . . . . knitting into front, back, then front again of same st (increase 2 sts)

k1-tbl . . . . knit 1 st through back loop

k2tog . . . . knit 2 sts together (decrease)

k2tog-tbl . . . . . knit 2 sts together through back loops

kwise . . . . knitwise (as if to knit)

LH . . . . left-hand

m(s) . . . . marker(s)

MC . . . . main color

mm . . . . millimeter(s)

M1 . . . . make 1 (increase)

M1k . . . . make 1 knitwise

M1p . . . . make 1 purlwise

pat(s) . . . . pattern(s)

p . . . . purl

p1f&b . . . . purl into front then back of same st (increase)

p1-tbl . . . . purl 1 st through back loop

p2tog . . . . purl 2 sts together (decrease)

pm . . . . place marker

psso . . . . pass slip st(s) over

pwise . . . . purlwise (as if to purl)

rem . . . . remain(s), remaining

rep(s) . . . . repeat(s), repeated, repeating

rnd(s) . . . . round(s)

RH . . . . right-hand

RS . . . . right side (of work)

rev sc . . . . reverse single crochet (crab st)

sc . . . . single crochet

sl . . . . slip, slipped, slipping

ssk . . . . [slip 1 st knitwise] twice from left needle to right needle, insert left needle tip into fronts of both slipped sts, knit both sts together from this position (decrease)

S2KP2 . . . . slip 2 sts as if to k2tog, k1, then pass the 2 slipped sts over the knit st—a centered double decrease

ssp . . . . [slip 1 st knitwise] twice from left needle to right needle, return both sts to left needle and purl both together through back loops

st(s) . . . . stitch(es)

St st . . . . stockinette stitch

tbl . . . . through back loop

tog . . . . together

w&t . . . . wrap next stitch then turn work (often used in short rows)

WS . . . . wrong side (of work)

wyib . . . . with yarn in back

wyif . . . . with yarn in front

yb . . . . yarn back

yf . . . . yarn forward

yo . . . . yarn over

* . . . . repeat instructions from *

( ) . . . . alternate measurements and/or instructions

[ ] . . . . instructions to be worked as a group a specified number of times

Yarn Sources

3 Kittens Needle Arts
750 Main Street, Suite 112
Mendota Heights, MN 55118
651-457-4969
www.3kittensneedlearts.com

Blackberry Ridge Woolen Mill
3776 Forshaug Road
Mt. Horeb, WI 53572
608-437-3762
www.blackberry-ridge.com

Cascade Yarns
www.cascadeyarns.com

Dale of Norway Yarns
www.dale.no/dalegarn

Homestead Heirlooms, LLC
www.homesteadheirlooms.com

Misti International
P.O. Box 2532
Glen Ellyn, IL 60138-2532
888-776-9276 (YARN)
www.mistialpaca.com

Raumagarn
Syvilla Tweed Bolson
512 Locust Road
Decorah, IA 52101
563-382-3711
email: smtweed@mchsi.com

Reynolds Yarns
JCA, Inc.
35 Scales Lane
Townsend, MA 01469
978-597-8794
www.jcacrafts.com

Standard Yarn Weight System

Categories of yarn, gauge ranges, and recommended needle and hook sizes

Yarn Weight Symbol & Category Names	0 Lace	1 Super Fine	2 Fine	3 Light	4 Medium	5 Bulky	6 Super Bulky
Type of Yarns in Category	Fingering 10 count crochet thread	Sock, Fingering, Baby	Sport, Baby	DK, Light Worsted	Worsted, Afghan, Aran	Chunky, Craft, Rug	Bulky, Roving
Knit Gauge Range* in Stockinette Stitch to 4 inches	33–40** sts	27–32 sts	23–26 sts	21–24 sts	16–20 sts	12–15 sts	6–11 sts
Recommended Needle in Metric Size Range	1.5–2.25 mm	2.25–3.25 mm	3.25–3.75 mm	3.75–4.5 mm	4.5–5.5 mm	5.5–8 mm	8 mm and larger
Recommended Needle U.S. Size Range	000 to 1	1 to 3	3 to 5	5 to 7	7 to 9	9 to 11	11 and larger
Crochet Gauge* Ranges in Single Crochet to 4 inch	32-42 double crochets**	21–32 sts	16–20 sts	12–17 sts	11–14 sts	8–11 sts	5–9 sts
Recommended Hook in Metric Size Range	Steel*** 1.6–1.4mm Regular hook 2.25 mm	2.25–3.5 mm	3.5–4.5 mm	4.5–5.5 mm	5.5–6.5 mm	6.5–9 mm	9 mm and larger
Recommended Hook U.S. Size Range	Steel*** 6, 7, 8 Regular hook B–1	B–1 to E–4	E–4 to 7	7 to I–9	I–9 to K–10½	K–10½ to M–13	M–13 and larger

* GUIDELINES ONLY: The above reflect the most commonly used gauges and needle or hook sizes for specific yarn categories.

** Lace weight yarns are usually knitted or crocheted on larger needles and hooks to create lacy, openwork patterns. Accordingly, a gauge range is difficult to determine. Always follow the gauge stated in your pattern.

*** Steel crochet hooks are sized differently from regular hooks--the higher the number, the smaller the hook, which is the reverse of regular hook sizing.

This Standards & Guidelines booklet and downloadable symbol artwork are available at: **YarnStandards.com**

Knitting References

Sisters Ingebjørg, Anne, and Gunhild Midtgarden on storehouse steps at the Midtgarden farm, Rauland, Telemark, Norway, 1890s.
GAUSTA COLLECTION,
VESTERHEIM ARCHIVE

Brunette, Cheryl. *Sweater 101: How to Plan Sweaters that Fit . . . and Organize Your Knitting Life at the Same Time.* Marrowstone Island, WA: Marrowstone Island Press, 2008.

Chatterton, Pauline. *Scandinavian Knitting Designs.* New York: Charles Scribner's Sons, 1977.

Martinson, Kate, "Scandinavian Nalbinding: Needle Looped Fabric", *Weavers Journal* XII, No. 2, Issue 45; Fall 1987.

McGregor, Sheila. *The Complete Book of Traditional Scandinavian Knitting.* New York: St. Martin's Press, 1984.

Shea, Terri. *Selbuvotter: Biography of a Knitting Tradition.* Seattle, WA: Spinningwheel LLC, 2007.

Sundbø, Annemor. *Everyday Knitting: Treasures from a Rag Pile.* Kristiansand, Norway: Torridal Tweed, 2000.

Swansen, Meg. *A Knitting Glossary DVD with Elizabeth Zimmermann and Meg Swansen.* Pittsville, WI: Schoolhouse Press, 2006.

Thomas, Mary. *Mary Thomas's Knitting Book.* New York: Dover, 1972.

Vogue Knitting: The Ultimate Knitting Book by the Editors of Vogue Knitting Magazine. New York: Sixth&Spring Books, 2002.

Williams, Joyce and Meg Swansen. *Armenian Knitting: Designs by Meg Swansen and Joyce Williams.* Pittsville, WI: Schoolhouse Press, 2008.

Historical References

Bethany Home Auxiliary, *Bethany Cook Book*, 1970.

Rømcke, Kirsten. *Idéhefte for Snorer & Bånd.* Oslo, Norway: Norges Husflidslag, 1982.

Stewart, Janice, and Janice S. Stewart. *The Folk Arts of Norway.* Rhinelander, Wisconsin: Nordhus Publishing, 1999.

Vesterheim Norwegian-American Museum. "WWII." *Vesterheim*, vol. 5, no. 2, 2007.

Vesterheim Norwegian-American Museum. "The Architecture of Immigration." *Vesterheim*, vol. 4, no. 1, 2006.

Wiman-Ringquist, Gia. *100 Landskaps-Vantar.* ICA Kuriren, 1982.

About the Photographers

Herbjørn Nilsen Gausta

Herbjørn Nilsen Gausta (1854–1924) was born in Vestfjorddalen, Telemark, Norway. In 1867, at the age of twelve, he immigrated with his parents and four sisters to Fillmore County in southeastern Minnesota. He attended Luther College in Decorah, Iowa, intending to become a teacher, but his interest in art led him away to Oslo and Munich to train as a painter.

Early in his art career, he traveled to Norway several times and stayed with family in Rauland, Telemark, while painting the Norwegian landscape. Most of these early paintings and preparatory sketches were destroyed in a fire in his Minneapolis studio in 1889. Soon after, he began to use photographs instead of sketches from which to paint.

The majority of the photographs in Vesterheim's collection were taken by Gausta in the 1890s. While being somewhat idyllic and artistically composed, his images are realistic in their depiction of domestic and agricultural life in both America and Norway.

Gausta did paint some of the scenes he had photographed, including his niece peeling apples and the old fisherman mending nets. In his day, Gausta was best known for the religious paintings he made to fit church altars. Today, his photographs can serve as a useful research tool for understanding daily life in rural Minnesota and rural Telemark.

Peter Julius Rosendahl

Peter Julius Rosendahl (1878–1942) was born near Spring Grove, Houston County, Minnesota. Peter's father, an immigrant from Hadeland, Norway, died in 1880, so Peter grew up in an extended family that included his mother, siblings, paternal grandmother, and maternal grandfather.

A farmer, he also took correspondence classes in mechanical and electrical engineering and then in art. In 1918, Peter sold his first cartoon strips to *Decorah-Posten*, a Norwegian-language newspaper published in Decorah, Iowa, but circulated widely throughout the Midwest. "Han Ola og han Per," a humorous series about Norwegian Americans, rural life, and the mechanical revolution, ran in the paper until 1935.

A large collection of glass-plate negatives taken by Peter Rosendal was donated to Vesterheim in 2002. The images depict the family, including his wife Othelia and their four children, and farm life in Houston County in the early twentieth century.

Acknowledgments

I love reading liner notes on CDs and records. I get nostalgic thinking that we are moving away from CDs now—what with those music devices that I still can't seem to get the hang of—I miss reading liner notes. Here are our versions of those old liner notes.

First we both need to thank Vesterheim and all the staff, who have been so kind and gracious to us during our foray into this crazy world of pattern writing and publishing.

Enormous thanks to Laurann Gilbertson, the textile curator at Vesterheim. She has been nothing but enthusiastic ever since the day we first started dreaming about this project. She provided us with access to everything Vesterheim has to offer. She also photographed all the artifacts for each project and assisted us in selecting the historical photos. She cheerfully provided many last-minute requests for photos and information as our deadline approached. Thanks, Laurann, you are a life saver!

We want to thank Kate Martinson. Kate, you have inspired us on so many levels, both personally and professionally. Your standing invitation to stay at your home made all those whirlwind trips to Decorah such a treat. It was great to have a cozy bed in which to crash and a friendly face to greet us each time we showed up at your doorstep. We thank you for your wonderful contributions to the book. Your students at Luther are so very lucky, and we feel lucky to have benefitted from your traveling classrooms ourselves. We are forever in awe of your commitment to fiber arts and its heritage.

We would like to thank Kari Cornell, our editor, for seeing beyond the initial ideas and recognizing the potential for this book. For you and everyone at Voyageur Press, we thank you so much.

Charlotte Quiggle, our technical editor, you are amazing! We are grateful for your attention to detail and dedication to the project. Knitters will appreciate the fact that you ensured each pattern was absolutely accurate, even if it meant we had to get up at 4 a.m. to review revision after revision.

Big thank yous to our test knitters and sample knitters: Diane Ritchy, Cathy Schmit, Shawn Jarvis, Tiffany Susens, Rachael Urban ... Oh, and Jenny Hystad—whose name do you have? (no, she wasn't a test knitter, just an inside joke).

To knitters everywhere, young and old, beginners and advanced: we cherish being a part of this great and wonderful community. You are the undeniable inspiration for this project in the first place.

Janine: First, I would like to thank my mother for always providing materials and projects for me. You are my true inspiration. I need to thank my grandmothers, Mary Malkovich and Isabel Kosel. I am proud to have come from women who did handwork out of necessity as well as for the love of doing it.

I need to thank some other special women also: Kathy Giuggio, Nancy Bussiere, and Val Sweeney, know that your support and faith in me has never gone unnoticed. You have all spurred me on in my endeavors and I am forever grateful.

I would like to mention a few others: Cis Mezin, Julie Mast, Laura Rasmussen, and all the girls at 3 Kittens Needle Arts, both co-workers and customers. The Giuggio family, the Foley family, the Pass family, the Clausens, the Roen family, the nanny brigade, Christopher Kosel, and Sherry McCrank—thanks to you all—I love you.

Last but certainly not least, I would like to give more than just my heartfelt thanks to Sue Flanders. Sue—what did we get ourselves into? I guess we're just two girls in over our heads with flink! Your friendship has meant so much to me this year. Here's to guilt-free knitting!

Sue: Thanks to my daughter, Alice, who put up with her mother dragging her to the woods for numerous photos sessions. Alice, thanks again for posting a request on your facebook page for a male to model the Voss sweaters. Thanks to Brennan Lunzer, who volunteered and did a great job, even though he had no idea what he was in for.

My deepest gratitude goes to my husband, Chuck, who supported me throughout this project. He kept things running while I was traveling, knitting, and writing. My standing order to him anytime we had to go anywhere was "You drive, I'll knit." What a trooper he was, putting up with pot pies and scrambled eggs when there was no time to cook.

Thanks to my dad, Jack Klein, for providing the chip carvings shown on pages 53, 65, and 98.

Thanks to my co-author, Janine. I always told her, "I would have never done this gigantic project without you", and it's true. We made great travel, research, designing, and knitting companions. We might have been in over our heads, but we sure had fun trying to keep above the tsunami of work. We also made the best out of each visit to Decorah—numerous trips through Rochester to John Hardy's BBQ, Syvilla's Tweeds and Fleeces, The Blue Heron Yarn Shop, and Vanberia Gifts—Decorah is a great and inspiring place!

Index